Collecting Sports Autographs

Tom Owens

Bonus Books, Inc., Chicago

To my parents, Ernie and Jeanette Owens, who always "loaned" me postage stamps for fan mail.

And to Diana Helmer, the woman who autographed my marriage license.

93 92 91 90 89   5 4 3 2 1

Library of Congress Catalog Card Number: 88-63167

International Standard Book Number: 0-933893-79-5

Bonus Books, Inc.
160 East Illinois Street
Chicago, Illinois 60611

Printed in the United States of America

Contents

Autographs Unite Fans and Players

C ongratulations! You've just started (or added to) a collection of sports autographs. Consider yourself an official autograph collector.

It might be possible to discuss why people collect autographs. Because you've started to read this book, you may have some ideas of your own. Instead, consider why both current and former players, along with other assorted sports personalities, *sign* autographs.

That's the real appeal of collecting autographs. When a player is depicted on a baseball card, he may pose for the picture, then that's it. Never again will he be directly linked with that card, even though millions of hobbyists may place that particular card in their collections. Autographs are a different story, however. In most cases, signing an autograph is a purely voluntary act, done without pay or other benefit. It is done as a personal gesture to say thanks for the support and encouragement of fans like you.

The key word here is *personal*. Even though the authentic signatures of a person may look the same, the circumstances behind the signature are always different.

Maybe a player scribbled a hurried signature only hours before participating in an historic sporting event. Perhaps the autograph is more formal and legible, after being signed in response to a fan mail request. In any case, an autograph is actual physical proof that a sports notable took a few seconds to reach out and individually acknowledge a fan.

If this is the first signature you've ever obtained, you may wonder how to go from here. *Collecting Sports Autographs* will help you decide the directions your hobby goals can take. First of all, the decision needs to be made on what not to collect.

Few (if any) autograph collectors would ever want to obtain one signature of every person who has ever participated in professional sports. Luckily, the nicest thing about autograph collecting is that no formal requirements exist. Hobbyists tailor their collections to their own sports interest. Some may collect autographs from only a certain team or era. Others will decide on a certain classification of players, such as Rookie of the Year award winners or pitchers who have thrown no-hitters. The most popular group of signatures collected is that of the baseball Hall of Famers.

This book also outlines some of the many types of collectibles which collectors try to get signed. Autographed trading cards are just one of several options. Some hobbyists will work for years trying to get an entire card set (often numbering more than 600 cards) signed. The chapter entitled "What Items Do I Get Autographed?" offers a detailed discussion of the alternatives.

Many newcomers to the hobby may wonder how collectors find celebrities to sign for them. Some new hobbyists get discouraged when they see retired baseball greats appearing at sports collectors conventions.

Babe Ruth was a willing autograph signer throughout his career, so many signed baseballs still exist from him today. Still, these collectibles can fetch $800 and up, due to the everlasting popularity of the Hall of Famer.

Collectors are faced with the problem of paying several dollars apiece to get a star's in-person autograph. But in many cases, other in-person and by-mail opportunities will exist to get those autographs you really want.

Don't worry if you live hundreds of miles from the nearest professional sports team. The chapter entitled "Creating Your Collection by Mail" provides information on how anyone can amass a collection solely with a few postage stamps, a few well-written letters and some imagination.

For the investor, autograph collecting can be profitable. Values of signatures skyrocket whenever a player dies or reaches a Hall of Fame. Consider the untimely death of Thurman Munson, the starting catcher for the New York Yankees throughout the 1970s. When a fatal plane crash prematurely ended Munson's career, autograph collectors realized they had waited too long to try

Former Orioles third baseman Brooks Robinson has to be one of the most gracious Hall of Famers living. He is friendly and considerate when making personal appearances, and he responds promptly to all fan mail. (Diana Helmer photo)

to get Munson to sign. Today, nearly every dealer will have baseball cards of Munson available. But try to find a dealer offering a Munson autograph at *any* price.

Think again about sports immortals like Joe DiMaggio, who now command fees surpassing $20,000 for signing autographs at hobby shows. Show promoters, in turn, charge up to $20 to obtain just one signature. DiMaggio was a willing signer by mail (at no cost) during the early 1980s. The challenge for collector-investors is knowing what signatures to obtain before superstardom hits the signers.

The excitement provided in collecting autographs is why an increasing number of collectors have lost interest in collecting baseball cards. The number of card-producing companies grows each year, as does the dozens of card sets which are produced. Some hobbyists are overwhelmed by the number of choices and the need to acquire thousands of cards each year. Autograph collecting, by contrast, gives hobbyists more personal freedom in finding what they really want to specialize in. No two autograph collections will ever look the same.

What follows in subsequent chapters will be lots of practical advice I've learned in my two decades as an autograph collector. Also, I've consulted many sports celebrities and other autograph collectors who've shared their observations on the hobby. Your experiences may be even different, because our hobby changes every day. Some current stars become stingy in their autographing habits, while other retired stars will suddenly welcome fan attention. Older legends will die and the supplies of their autographs will become scarce, but new, young sports hopefuls will appear on the horizon and give collectors new names to add to their collections.

No matter what, one thing about our hobby will remain the same. Any time a hobbyist acquires a sports signature, be it in person, by mail or through a dealer, that hobbyist has obtained a very small part of that personality's life.

That's what makes collecting sports autographs special.

What Items Do I Get Autographed?

2

Before approaching a sports celebrity for an autograph (be it face to face or through the mail), every collector must decide one important question: what item should the celebrity autograph?

This question is often overlooked by fans who may be only casual collectors. Some of these followers of fame may argue that any autograph is a worthwhile acquisition. But how many of these half-hearted hobbyists will display an autographed matchbook cover or a signed hot dog wrapper in their homes?

Furthermore, athletes "know the score" among collectors. If sports stars take the time to sign an autograph for someone, it's done with the hope that the recipient will preserve and treasure the signature. To the people who may sign their names for others dozens of times through the day, bits of paper and other incidental items don't seem like autographable possessions. In these cases, many a player will only oblige serious collectors who have serious collectibles ready for signing.

"I wouldn't sign skin," says Bob Randall, former Minnesota Twins second baseman and current baseball

One of the most popular choices of autograph collectors today is the signed 8-by-10 photo. These are readily available from dealers and at shows where the personality is appearing. However, a few players refuse to sign "unauthorized" photos not licensed by Major League Baseball. These players claim that they receive no profit from sales of these photos and decline to autograph them.

coach at Iowa State University. "I'd sign gloves, baseballs, cards, photos, and more personal things like that." Such feelings seem typical among today's players. Often, superstar athletes who are chided for not signing

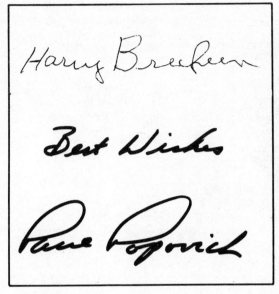

Compare the two signatures. Harry Brecheen, a 1950s pitching star, used a mere ballpoint pen to sign his autograph. Paul Popovich, a utility infielder in the late 60s and early 70s, used a Sharpie permanent marker to create a bolder signature. See the differences?

autographs usually base their excuses on beliefs that fans usually throw away the signatures after they are received.

To counteract this skepticism among athletes, collectors who have time to prepare for in-person autographs hunts can select personal items for autographs. Trading cards are popular choices for any major sports collection. They are small, easy to handle and display, and quite informative. I was able to have a short, pleasant conversation with Houston Astros coach Denis Menke last season, due to our common Iowa childhoods. How did I know about Menke's past? By reading the backs of his baseball cards!

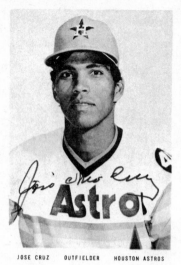

Many teams furnish photos to players who want them for personal appearances, or for fan mail responses. It never hurts to ask a player to include a photo with his reply. Many will happily!

JOSE CRUZ   OUTFIELDER   HOUSTON ASTROS

Collectors who may meet an entire team at its motel or leaving the stadium can use a shortcut in getting various cards signed. Instead of trying to leaf through a large stack of cards in a second's notice, it's possible to display several cards at once in a scrapbook, mounting them by adhesive photo corners. This method doesn't damage cards. Best of all, a collector can open a scrapbook page and have a star sign several cards in a flash. Hurried players enjoy this route, because they can use the smooth and sturdy writing surface of the scrapbook and they never have to handle each one of the cards they sign.

Don't overlook minor league and college cards. Future stars are delighted to see early pictures of themselves, knowing that fans have supported them even in their less successful beginnings.

Player photographs are nice collectibles to have

signed, too. They are available in various forms, ranging from sets of postcard-sized photos offered by many teams to glossy, full-color 8-by-10s now sold by many hobby dealers. Baseball teams make a sincere effort to provide some type of photos of all team members for the public. A club like the New York Mets has stunning full-color postcards of all team members available each season. The cards aren't sold anywhere. They're provided to players for their own personal use (especially to use when answering fan mail). Others are used for promotional purposes by the front office. Teams like the San Francisco Giants sell 8-by-10s (black and white) for $3 each. Football and basketball teams usually prefer 8-by-10s, too.

Check with your favorite team for availability of photos. They're affordable and look great autographed. I've personally met lots of rookies and just-traded players outside of stadiums and in hotel lobbies. Their look of disappointment from signing generic items like program covers and index cards disappears when a fan can provide an actual photo to be signed. Even minor league teams and colleges sometimes have photos to sell, so it's worth exploring. I've found that many pro franchises will even send a free photo when an inquiry about just one favorite player has been made.

Many hobby dealers have discovered the demand for player photographs. During a recent visit to the Kansas City Sports Collectors Convention, I was amazed to see that one in every three hobby dealers present had different color photos of Brooks Robinson and Lou Brock (special guests appearing to sign autographs at the show). The average price for an 8-by-10 photo was $2.50. All of these were professionally-posed photos, many of them vintage shots from the younger days of both Hall of Famers.

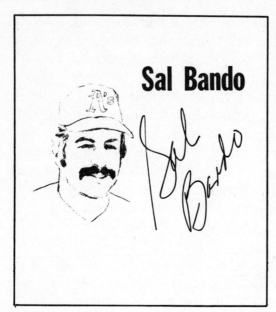

There are many ways to make blank index cards more appealing. Then the player may appreciate your efforts and be more willing to answer your fan letter.

Some photos and trading cards aren't that receptive to being autographed. Ballpoint pens can't sign on the slick surface of many cards and photos. Autograph signers sometimes have to literally carve their names into the surface with the pen. Felt-tip pens produce light and hazy impressions.

To solve the problem, try using the Sharpie permanent marker, available for less than $1 at most stationery and office supply stores. Sharpies come in assorted colors, which can be coordinated with specific photos to produce perfect color schemes. Collector purists stick solely with blue Sharpie signatures. The Sharpie

Team sheets are single pages signed by the members of one team. The Arkansas Travelers minor league baseball team (the class AA affiliate for the St. Louis Cardinals) signed this one. The logo is from a sticker found in a pack of Fleer baseball cards. Several of these players have reached the majors now, and getting their autographs might be tougher than it was when they were unnoticed by most fans and collectors in the minors.

becomes a magic wand for collectors, who suddenly can have nearly anything signed, including odd treasures like bats and jerseys. These amazing writing instruments will create bold signatures on any surface, excluding baseballs. Sharpie ink "bleeds" on baseballs.

Signatures get runny and faded on such leather.

Speaking of baseballs, these little cowhide spheres are becoming a hot property among collectors. Some collectors will want only one signature on each ball. Other fans will try for entire teams. I've seen balls with as many as 30 autographs! Veteran hobbyists get only star players to sign the "sweet spot" on a baseball, which is the blank horizontal area opposite the insignia and between the two sets of stitches. This extra room allows for a large, dynamic autograph. Team baseball collectors like to have a manager's signature on this space.

Sporting goods stores offer "official" American and National League baseballs at $6 to $7 each. These are the same balls used in league play. The baseballs even have the facsimile signatures of the respective league presidents on them. When it comes to resale value, an official ball will command as much as 25 percent more than other signed balls.

Footballs and basketballs aren't as popular with many autograph collectors. Why? Try fitting three dozen of either type of ball on your living room shelves. Then you'll realize that storage and display problems discourage most hobbyists. Even smaller objects like hockey pucks or golf balls haven't swept the hobby because their rough surfaces don't invite autographs.

Baseballs, however, are more compact. Various display accessories are available to showcase signed baseballs, with costs as little as $3 per ball-holder. A new product called a Ballqube is sold in many hobby outlets. This inventive lucite case allows signed balls to be stacked, and all autographed sides of the baseball can be viewed at once. See the chapter entitled "How to Display Your Collection" for more hints.

Choosing possible items for autographing may

seem easy, especially if a collector simply plans to send them to the designated signer directly. Getting items signed in person can be trickier. Seeing players wearing uniforms with names and numbers attached makes life simple for hobbyists. But when those players are wearing civilian attire outside stadiums or in hotel lobbies, identification may become troublesome. By the time a collector may fish out a photo of a certain player from the pile, a half-dozen team members may have departed the scene.

A practical solution is found in the white index card. Commonly called a "3-by-5" in the hobby in reference to its size, the index card has another function besides filling up a recipe box. Collectors do use 3-by-5s to gain signatures of team members who seem unrecognizable. Believe me, almost any player will turn sour after being mistaken for a teammate. Most pro athletes hope that the public will know their faces. This potential disaster can be avoided by politely handing an index card to the unknown player and asking to have it signed. Experienced collectors prefer index cards signed on the unlined side.

Mailing index cards for autograph requests can provide unexpected bonuses. As long as you enclose a self-addressed, stamped envelope with your letter, many sports personalities will return a photo to an index card collector upon request. When I can't find a picture of a certain player, I'll write and explain that I'd like to have his photo to add to my collection. I'd say that one of every seven athletes responds to my request when they reply.

Index cards don't have to look boring. Some fans may glue small photos of players on the cards. Other collectors may type lifetime statistics of the player on the card to make the 3-by-5 more personal. This works best when sending out the card by mail, because most celebrities are impressed with the effort you've spent in pursuing their signatures.

Another homemade creation I enjoy getting autographs on is a team sheet. This idea came to me when I grew frustrated with my inability to fill my apartment with autographed baseballs. Instead, I took sheets of typing paper and mounted a team sticker in the center of each. Team stickers are available free or at a cost of 25 cents or less from a club's front office. For baseball teams, I like to use the stickers enclosed in wax packs of Fleer baseball cards. (Few people actually collect the stickers, so they have little to no resale value.)

I'll put my team sheet on a clipboard and pass it about when I meet a group of players. The flat backing of the clipboard makes signing a breeze. Soon, I have a beautiful signature-filled sheet ready to be framed. On an ongoing basis, I add autographs to my "team theme" sheets. Whenever I meet former St. Louis Cardinals at a show or ballpark, I'll have them sign the sheet. Soon, I'll have a fascinating mixture of autographs of Cardinal old-timers.

Although tastes differ, I've never enjoyed getting sports books signed. Some hobbyists like to get players to sign their designated page in a yearbook or baseball encyclopedia. This may be challenging, but it's hard to view each autograph regularly without rifling through the book's pages. When this is done, the collectible suffers needless wear and tear (and the value declines).

If I was trapped on a desert island with the entire Chicago Cubs team and nothing but a yearbook to get autographs on, I'd ask each player to sign the book's cover. That way, at least, all the signatures could be seen together.

An even bigger temptation for collectors is getting signed sports biographies. When a bookstore announces that some sports superstars will be signing copies of their life story at the store, fans flock to the scene. Granted, it may be a rare opportunity to get a star's autograph, but how can the signature be displayed? Does a collector point to a shelf and tell others that an autograph is tucked deep inside that book? No thanks! I'd rather spread my signed treasures across the walls or shelves of my house and in secure albums that can be viewed easily, so the autographs can be shared with other admirers.

The last variable in choosing what collectibles are best for autographing relates to value. If a collector wants autographed items which could later be sold for top prices, I'd suggest avoiding autographed cards.

It's fun to try to get an entire set of cards autographed. But trying to get Hank Aaron or some other superstar to sign a valuable card simply to increase its worth is risky. Non-autograph oriented collectors might scoff at a signed Aaron card. Their premise is that cards should be in pristine mint condition, untainted by any creases or markings, including an autograph.

Autographs gained for investment purposes should be on baseballs or color photos. I saw collectors in attendance at a 1988 St. Louis hobby show double their money in an hour. Ex-Boston Red Sox star Ted Williams was a guest signer, but his autographs cost $15 a pop. Undaunted hobbyists would buy three or more Williams autograph tickets and get the "Splendid Splinter" to sign three official American League balls. With a total investment of no more than $22 per ball, these fans could find other collectors in attendance who'd pay $35 to $40 for that signed ball instantly.

Whatever type of mementos a hobbyist wants to build an autograph collection with is fine, as long as the hobby is pursued for fun. Be it cards, photos, baseballs or other collectibles, the important part is that the items, both signed and unsigned, have special meaning to you, the autograph collector.

Finding the
Celebrity Signers

3

"Can I have your autograph?"
It's possible to ask that question in more places than ever before, as both current and former sports notables become more visible in today's society.

The average fan might believe that the only option for autograph collectors is seeking out players at sporting events. This isn't as simple as it sounds. Supposing an athlete spots you in the stands after you've shouted, waved and begged for an autograph. At that very moment, 50 other sports fans and two ushers may race you to that athlete. What you thought would be a simple meeting turns into a pro wrestling match. Even if you avoid other fans, security personnel may try to chase you back to your seat. They want to discourage unruly mobs from rushing onto a field. Some ushers may feel like they need to protect players from maniacs.

A simple pregame signing can go haywire quickly. During a 1988 trip to Dodger Stadium in Los Angeles, for instance, I saw fans young and old clamoring by the dugout for a signature from star pitcher Fernando Valenzuela. A security guard squatted on the dugout

During a 1988 old-timer's game at Dodger Stadium, fans had a chance to get autographs from accomplished past players like Tommy Davis. However, getting autographs at stadiums before a game is hectic and unpredictable with lots of competition. (Photo by Tot Holmes)

roof to stop overzealous youngsters from leaping onto the field. One young fan, though, nearly caused a riot when he underhanded a ball to Valenzuela to be signed. The Dodger hurler didn't see the ball sailing toward him in the sun, and he got bonked on the head. A team coach screamed into the stands, fearing that his key player was injured. The embarrassed usher seemed prepared to eject the youngster. Fernando, meanwhile, used the confusion as a way to escape into the dugout and avoid signing for anyone else.

After a game, many fans will camp out in stadium parking lots waiting for departing players to sign. A game-winning hero may stop and greet fans, but the athlete responsible for single-handedly losing the game may delight in shunning autograph seekers. Other players may leave without signing, just because their stint at work is done and they want to go home. This routine is only for the most patient of collectors. Hours of standing around waiting for the players to appear can be fruitlessly over in seconds.

Many saner, easier alternatives exist for prospective collectors who feel that game autograph seeking is too unpredictable and time-consuming. The unpredictability may be what excites many veteran hobbyists. But even the most seasoned collectors will agree that getting an autograph shouldn't be a frustrating, unrewarding experience.

Teams and players alike know that they can't always find the time to sign thousands of autographs at a time. Despite the impossibility of giving signatures to every fan in the stands before a game, some critics blast players as heartless and arrogant for passing up even one autograph seeker. To avoid such unwarranted criticism, most pro teams will organize weekly signing sessions before specially-designated home games. These sessions are usually promoted beforehand, but few teams can announce which players are recruited for signing duties until the last minute. That's okay, because many teams will provide photos for players to pass out at these free signings, so collectors don't have to scramble to find their own items to be autographed. Because players don't have lots of free time immediately before a game, these sessions may last only an hour or less (and can't completely satisfy the demand for autographs). But wise fans who are prepared can usually cash in on these free events. Try calling the community service or promotions department of your favorite club before you attend your next game for details and ground rules.

Collectors will treat a professional team like royalty when it plays on home turf. But when those players

go on the road, they're often overlooked in favor of local
heroes. A wise collector will try to locate visiting team
members at their official hotel before or after games. A
couple of young autograph hounds from Kansas City
said that they seldom see more than three or four other
hobbyists greeting some visiting teams at their K.C. hotels, while consistent, well-known winning clubs like
the New York Yankees may attract up to 50 autograph
hunters at once. Still, those 50 people know that an additional 5,000 fans might be standing in line for signatures when the team arrives at the ballpark.

But don't think that the staff of a metropolitan hotel
puts up with rowdy hobbyists chasing athletes up and
down lobbies in search of autographs. Most hotels will
eject everyone but registered guests from the lobby. Patient collectors, however, will camp outside the front
door and wait for the players as they leave for (or return
from) the stadium.

Paying guests get lots more flexibility when it
comes to player access. Chicago collector Rick Firfer
says that his two sons enjoyed Christmas in July when
they stayed at the same Cincinnati hotel which
hosted members of the 1988 Major League Baseball
All-Star teams. As long as they had a room key for
identification, the youngsters had no problems.
Meanwhile, unlucky fans staying elsewhere were
told by hotel management that they'd have to hunt
autographs *outside*.

Incredibly, information on out-of-town lodging locations for pro teams isn't a secret. Teams will provide
this information in their preseason information guides
to assist the media (but these press guides are now sold
to the public). It seems that a fan could gain the same information by calling the public relations department of

Unlike the confined atmosphere of a stadium, fans attending spring training can get within inches of stars. Here, Dodgers coach and Hall of Famer Sandy Koufax happily greeted hordes of supporters at Dodgertown in Vero Beach, Florida, in 1988. (Photo by Tot Holmes)

a club. Teams realize that it's exciting for fans to stay only one floor below two dozen sports personalities.

Another free smorgasbord for autograph hounds is at preseason training camps for pro teams. The best known happenings of this sort are baseball's spring training or football's late summer workout sites. Not even half of the average regular-season crowds will be on hand seeking autographs in the preseason. Athletes stay more relaxed and interested in fan interaction, because the daily pressure to win hasn't started yet. Sometimes it's even possible to have a brief conversation with a player who isn't swamped with autograph requests.

The nice part about preseason camps is that players may be around for more than just exhibition games. Some may take part in drills or practices, and others may be simply lounging around the premises. In the case of baseball's spring training in Florida, fans are able to team hop from locale to nearby locale, visiting the sites of several major league teams in only a week. The only tricky part about preseason workouts is that teams don't always require veteran athletes to participate in all games. Some baseball stars will depart by the fourth inning of spring training games. It's good to question veteran collectors in attendance about the work tendencies of certain players if you're pursuing one special signature.

Don't overlook additional stars who may be with a team during its preseason training. In baseball, Hall of Famers like Sandy Koufax and Bob Feller serve as coaches during spring training but not during the regular season. Non-sports celebrities may pop up, too. Country music singer Charley Pride works out yearly with the Texas Rangers.

Once again, team media guides are good sources for this information. By sending a self-addressed, stamped envelope to a team's ticket office, it's possible to get a schedule listing a club's preseason plans. Florida and Arizona heavily publicize baseball spring training locales each year, while states like Wisconsin do the same regarding their pro football training camps. Teams freely share the information because tickets are sold to many preseason games.

All of these possibilities involve a little luck and a lot of planning. Still, no guarantees exist that any player will sign autographs for you. These ideas do beat the previously discussed methods of battling the masses usually at stadiums during the regular season. But the surest thing for a collector who craves the autograph of one particular star is to attend a hobby show.

Each week all across the country, collector conventions of varying sizes are being held in settings ranging from church basements and American Legion halls to large hotel convention centers and city auditoriums. At almost all of these gatherings, show promoters will hire either current or former players to attend and sign autographs. These celebrity guest signers are high-powered drawing cards who attract additional hundreds of attendees to events once frequented by only small groups of dedicated hobbyists.

How does getting autographs at hobby shows work? The collector pays an admission fee (which can range from 50 cents to $5) to get into the show. After paying admission, collectors usually have to pay another fee (known as an autograph ticket). Each ticket entitles the collector to one signature from the guest signer. Autograph fees may range from a dollar or two for a lesser-known retired player to $15 to $20 for a superstar or Hall of Fame personality such as baseball's Ted Williams or Joe DiMaggio, or boxing's Muhammad Ali.

When irate fans balk at paying so much just for the right to acquire one mere mortal's signature, it's an impulse to condemn the stars who are signing for such big bucks. "How can Eric Davis and Mark McGwire charge so much for their autographs when they make so much money playing baseball?" some critics might charge. Well, the guest signers usually get paid before their appearance starts. It's the decision of the show promoter regarding the fees charged to show attendees for each autograph. Some promoters may try to charge collectors only enough money to cover expenses when hiring guests. Others may hope to make a few thousand dollars from autograph signings during the festivities. Even non-collectors will, in a sense, pay for the hobby show appearance of an athletic celebrity. Admission, which simply allows a person entrance to the location where the show is held, can cost as much as $5 apiece if several baseball superstars appear.

Actually, many sports stars might not care at all about the fees charged for their signatures. Show promoters pay their guest stars beforehand, sometimes on an hourly rate, other times based on a maximum number of signatures to be signed that day. So, at two cents or $20 per autograph ticket, the guest signer will still get the same amount of money.

However, don't think that the sometimes hurried, business-like behavior of athletes at hobby shows is done at their own choosing. In fact, many show promoters who want to accommodate more than 1,000 paying customers in one afternoon may put restrictions on the guest's behavior. Some promoters may forbid guests from signing personalized autographs, shaking hands or posing for pictures with fans.

Which shows are the best to attend to get autographs from guests? Or what guests are the most friendly to their fans who come to see them at shows? It depends. The easiest way to know what shows to attend for autographs can be accomplished by calling or writing the show promoter beforehand. What restrictions are placed on their celebrity guests? How many hours (and how many days) will the guest appear? Any professional show promoter should be willing to answer these questions in advance.

In the case of knowing which guests to go see, that's a tougher challenge. Baseball immortals like Pete Rose and Mantle have gotten both hisses and hurrahs for their behavior at different shows. Celebrities are people, too. They may simply have a bad day. At other times, their differing treatment by show promoters may influence their signing performances. Then again, some stars harbor more universal resentment toward signing for pay. They seem to want the money, but they are determined not to enjoy the effort it takes.

The public discovered the autographing attitudes of former San Francisco Giant Willie Mays in June 1988, during an autograph appearance at a bookstore to promote his biography. According to various press reports, Mays demanded $10 per autograph from people who wouldn't buy a copy of his book to be signed. A young boy hoping for a free autograph began to cry when he realized he couldn't afford the price.

Such reports were old news to veteran hobbyists who had tried to get a signature from Mays at hobby shows. Many collectors have told me that Mays sports a contrary stubborn streak at all of his show appearances. Asking Mays to use a certain type of pen to sign with, or asking for a signature in a certain spot on a collectible will only get opposite results. When *Sports Collectors Digest* reporter David Craft tried to interview former manager Leo Durocher at a St. Louis card show, fellow guest signer Mays tried to stop the conversation, insisting that his ex-skipper should get paid for speaking to the press.

The hobby press, especially publications like *Sports Collectors Digest* and *Baseball Card News*, are valuable sources to discover the current habits of guest signers. (See the appendix for subscription information.) Getting to know an experienced collector is another helpful way to find the best in-person signers.

The media can guide collectors to other opportunities to meet current and former players, although many of these events may be tougher than other options previously discussed. Store openings, public lectures, golf tournaments, charity or club banquets and church services may be only a few public happenings where a sports notable could be met. Granted, thousands of other collectors may not be competing for elbow room with you. An even greater number of non-collectors, however, may decide to get their first (and last) autograph ever, simply because it's a trendy thing to do.

An example of this happened to me during the 1987 American Legion World Series banquet in Stevens Point, Wisconsin. After the banquet, hundreds of attendees jumped up and rushed to get autographs of former baseball stars like Jay Johnstone, Pete Vuckovich, Rollie Fingers, Andy Pafko and Sal Bando. I avoided the jostling partly because I knew I'd have little luck getting a signature when hundreds of other people wanted the same thing. But I didn't have to.

I did my homework before the event. I read the local sports page and I called the local promoter. A last-minute free autograph signing session was planned earlier that evening. I slipped in then and got all the signatures I wanted before the crowds swooped down. The session was peaceful and unhurried. Here, former stars who might cost anywhere from $4 to $8 for a single autograph during a hobby show appearance were signing for nothing. Pafko, a star from the 1950s, sat practically unnoticed by the young crowd of American Legion players and their families.

Finally, remember to enlist family, friends and strangers in your autograph searches. In the mid-1970s, my parents took me for a summer vacation to Cooperstown, New York, to view the National Baseball Hall of Fame and Museum. We stayed at a small inn on the outskirts of town, across the road from Lake Otsego. After my father told the innkeeper that his two sons wished they could get some autographs from all the famous players enshrined in the hall, the innkeeper had an alternative idea.

She pointed across the road to a man sitting in a fishing boat with a few friends. This angler was none other than Jim Konstanty, the heroic relief pitcher for the 1950 Philadelphia Phillies "Whiz Kids" team. Konstanty, happy to be recognized as a former player, signed some index cards and shared some stories of his past accomplishments. Later that week, we met Vernon "Whitey" Wilshire, a local resident who had pitched for the Philadelphia Athletics. We reaped the benefits of two delightful coincidences, merely because we weren't shy about discussing our hobby with anyone.

Remember, discovering the whereabouts of current and former athletes who will sign autographs isn't that difficult. With a little patience and determination, any fan's search for stars can yield both autographs and happy memories.

Creating Your Collection by Mail

4

Too many people give up quickly as autograph collectors. Granted, it can be discouraging to be ignored by a famous athlete who is only inches away from signing your favorite photo. Or the idea of standing in line for an hour and paying $8 to get a quick signature from a Hall of Famer might seem crazy to sane fans.

But a painless, inexpensive option exists. All it takes is a little patience, a lot of creativity and a few postage stamps. That's right! Almost any professional athlete, current or former, can be approached by mail. A short, polite and personal letter can make the difference with almost any sports celebrity.

How is this possible? It works, with the use of a secret weapon: the self-addressed, stamped envelope (SASE). All this means is that you send an unsealed envelope with your address and proper return postage so the celebrity can reply easily. With a SASE, it's possible to sign the enclosed items quickly, shove them in the furnished envelope and mail away the response. Baseball Hall of Fame star Enos "Country" Slaughter proudly told an interviewer once that fan mail, when accompanied by a SASE, gets returned in less than three days in most instances.

Former New York Yankees teammate and fellow baseball Hall of Fame star Johnny "the Big Cat" Mize explains the need for a SASE with this story: "Once I got a letter from a dentist," he says. "All it said was, 'Please send two autographed photos for me and my son.' I felt like writing back to ask if he'd fix my teeth for free."

Mize has a point. Few current players, let alone retired ones, get money from their teams to pay for correspondence with fans. At 25 cents a stamp, a current star with thousands of fans could lose a large chunk of cash quickly. Besides, a collector lucky enough to receive a few minutes of a player's time shouldn't expect free postage as well.

Wise collectors won't try to sidestep the courtesy rules of collecting. Those hobbyists who enclose only a stamp but not an envelope may never see a response from the celebrity. Famous players don't have lots of free time. Do you think they'd want to spend it addressing 300 envelopes per week?

I asked Tom Brunansky, who was traded from the Minnesota Twins to the St. Louis Cardinals in 1988, how much fan mail (autograph requests) he received directly after his move. "Too much!" he said, only half-jokingly. He went on to explain that he didn't have any help sorting the letters (many from well-wishing Twins fans) and that the change of scenery had sidetracked his signing habits. Philadelphia Phillies star Mike Schmidt often takes a year to sign a fan mail request, so it's easy to guess that he receives tons of letters annually.

Another dubious shortcut some newer collectors try is the mass mailing. In an attempt to save some postage, one enormous package will be mailed to a team's clubhouse. The collector assumes that some amiable team employee will open the package and sort all the letters and different items for players to sign, then distribute the correspondence. Not so! Few if any team public relations departments will assign any employee to such a mundane task. After all, such a fan demand is akin to the electric company sending one packet of utility bills to one apartment dweller and then expecting the tenant to distribute more bills to 24 neighbors in the building.

When writing to a player, make it short. That doesn't mean to send a telegram, but suggests that one-page letters are best. A fan might enjoy writing a comprehensive, multi-page greeting to an athlete, but will page after page hold a stranger's attention? After all, an autograph request letter should convince the reader why the letter-writer deserves an autograph. Long-winded messages won't do, especially if that same star receives 200 other letters from fans each week. That's the number Hall of Famer and Baltimore Orioles manager Frank Robinson says he gets each week.

Even though your letter is short, see that it is personal. Don't feel the need to pour out your heart on paper. Just show the recipient that this same letter isn't being sent to hundreds of other players at the same time.

Try sharing a personal memory of seeing an athlete play. It's a good way to form an instant relationship with that player. I recalled seeing former Cardinals third baseman Ken Reitz play in the low minors years ago. I wrote and told him this, so he returned a photo (of his own) which was signed "To Tom, a fan who followed my career from the start to the present." This personal touch in a letter doesn't have to be empty flattery. Even players can distinguish compliments from cowpies.

If a player starred before you were even born, write and say that you've read about him. Recite a little-known fact that impressed you about the player's career. If these players never cracked the starting lineup, mention that you admire how athletes can be part-time stars. If you're writing to a rookie, send your best wishes for the future.

Be honest. Admit why you really wrote to an athlete. If you want to collect the signatures of all ex-Brooklyn Dodgers, say so. Even a mediocre player of the past will be proud of belonging to such a unique team from baseball history. But phrase your request so that a player still feels special and admired. An ex-player may have little motivation to sign for you if he feels that you've been contacting thousands of retirees at random with no concern about their individual careers.

Be specific. Past and present players have set goals throughout their careers. Knowing that you, as a collector, have a goal may gain the cooperation of some stubborn signers. Pitcher Mike Marshall, a notorious non-signer, relented on occasion while with the Minnesota Twins. If some collectors told him they wanted him to sign a baseball only to complete their team collection, he'd comply.

Above all, be polite. An unruly letter with many demands will get ignored, and will help sour a once-willing signer on the whole hobby. A former Cardinals outfielder says he receives some photocopied form letters reading "Dear ----," with the player's name added sloppily at the last minute. Joe Garagiola, noted sports announcer, says that he's most convinced by hand-written letters composed on lined paper.

But don't be shy. If you want your cards signed on

JERRY TERRELL - Twins

Many religious players like to make their personal autographs more personalized. Some, like Jerry Terrell, like to add their favorite Bible verse to their signature.

their fronts, specify your need. Back-signed trading cards are tough to display. It's nicer to see both a photo and signature on the same side at the same time.

It's considered proper to request a short personalization when requesting an autograph by mail. Former Golden State Warriors star Rick Barry did just that for me. Personalized autographs have a lower resale value, but they provide more meaning for the collector.

Also, ask if the player has any extra photos, and if he'd be willing to include one in his reply. I've found that one out of every seven players who reply to my letters will enclose one of their own photos upon request. Some even have religious tracts printed up, which offer their photo and their personal Christian testimony together in one pamphlet.

Don't be greedy, though. If you enclose more than three items, many celebrities suspect that you might want to keep just one and sell the rest. If you enclose more than one card or photo without a special explanation, see that the items are different. As a young collector, I sent five or six items to a few players, and received only three of my cards back in return. However, if collectors have one or two duplicate cards, it's polite to enclose them in the letter with an offer for the player to keep them if desired.

Asking a player to personalize a signature is a reasonable request. A simple notation, such as "To Tom and Diana" isn't unreasonable. In fact, point out that your desire for a personalized autograph proves that you don't plan on selling your signed treasures. Why would anyone named George want a photo inscribed with another person's name?

These are acceptable requests to make. Trying to interview a player in a letter isn't so practical. If Reggie Jackson gets thousands of fan letters each year, it would be admirable if he managed to sign and return an autograph (let alone an essay) to each writer.

Yet, lesser-known retired players who weren't accustomed to daily interviews may be thrilled to answer a fan. I asked an ex-White Sox pitcher, Paul LaPalme, how he felt about Al Lopez, his former manager, making it to the Hall of Fame. For Hal Naragon, I inquired about Bill Veeck, his one-time team owner and boss. I wrote to former St. Louis Brown Jim Delsing to get his thoughts on appearing as a guest signer at a local card show. All responded with one-paragraph replies.

Simpler "yes or no" types of short answer questions might work best with recent players. Who was their favorite manager? Do they collect baseball cards? Do they like the designated hitter rule? The possibilities are endless.

Back when computerized All-Star game ballots were offered to baseball fans, I'd send ballots to different players to get their opinions. They'd simply punch out a few boxes and return it to me signed. For them, it was quick, easy and fun.

Finally, offer in writing to serve the player in return. Offer, in appreciation, to help the player acquire some extra cards of himself. You may be surprised with the results. Dave Niven of Brick, New Jersey, says that Indians star Cory Snyder sought several extra cards for his family. Not only will a sincere offer help get a quicker reply from a celebrity, it could bring an additional thrill by assisting someone famous.

Before you sign your letter, say thanks. Plus, when you get a surprise reply of extra photos, personalizations or other nice touches, consider sending another postcard of appreciation to the player to show your gratitude. Any time a collector receives an autograph in the mail from an athlete, it is sent because that player wanted to acknowledge the encouragement fans like you provide.

That autograph you received is a personal way of saying that you make a difference.

Meet Jack Smalling,   <u>5</u>
Hobby Detective

To most people around the central Iowa university community of Ames, Jack Smalling is known as an insurance salesman, high school sports referee and a former semi-pro baseball player.

But to many veteran hobbyists, Jack Smalling is a pioneer in the autograph collecting hobby.

Never mind that Smalling has a collection which approaches 10,000 *different* major league signatures. Forget that he only started his collection in 1962, after pursuing nothing but baseball cards for 23 years. What makes Smalling so special to the autograph collecting hobby is *The Baseball Address List.*

Now co-authored with Maryland sports memorabilia dealer Denny Eckes, this list is more like an encyclopedia for autograph hounds wanting to contact their favorite past or present baseball stars at their home addresses by mail. More than 25,000 hobbyists purchased the fourth edition of Smalling's book, a figure likely to grow following the September 1988 release of the fifth paperback edition.

Smalling first tinkered with the idea of publishing a

baseball player home address directory in 1964. His first effort was a mere collection of mimeographed sheets of addresses stapled together. Previously, he had found some success looking up the hometowns of players through *Street and Smith's Baseball Yearbook*. He'd write to the various players, all living in small towns, simply in care of their local post offices and the mail deliverers would do the rest. Smalling laughs and says that a collector would have little, if any, success writing to anyone today without knowing a proper street address.

Incredibly, an old Cincinnati Reds team yearbook provided Smalling with his first home addresses for current players. Back then, the team actually published the information, and Smalling found that he got more autographs by writing to the Reds at their homes. It seems that major league teams were much more fan-oriented in the past.

Smalling's first autographs came in the mail from the 1955 Chicago Cubs. "The Cubs front office wrote back and said to send a postcard with my name and address on it. Then they'd have the player sign it and mail it back to me. So, I sent in a whole stack of them and got them back," Smalling says. "Of course, that's when postcards were just three cents apiece."

Smalling's current address list includes more than 10,000 entries. The list is arranged alphabetically. Each entry provides a debut year (dating from 1910 through 1987) and a code number which helps Smalling document the number of players who debuted that season. (He also uses the code number to quickly list the number of autographs he has for sale at any given time.) He will list a current mailing address for each person (umpires and coaches with no major league playing experience get special sections in the book). Occasionally, no

Hall of Famer Don Drysdale signs an autograph for sportscaster Joe Garagiola at a 1988 old-timer's game. Garagiola, a veteran major leaguer himself, is also a long-time hobbyist. (Photo by Tot Holmes)

current address will be available for a player. In these cases, Smalling will list the last known mailing address.

"The book is 90 percent accurate," Smalling says, "which is very good, considering that 20 percent of the population moves yearly." In the past, relatively unknown players, such as Joe Hague, Bill Singer, Rich Reese, Joey Jay, Paul Casanova, Mike Kekich or Wes Covington have eluded Smalling's searches. "There's only so many hours in the day, and you can't be looking for players all the time," he says, adding that he has used a computer for several years to help track such investigations. Smalling speculates that lesser-known players are more easily forgotten by the public, so current addresses sometimes are forgotten. "Sometimes, I think these guys don't want to be found by fans," he adds.

The case of Covington, a former outfielder for the Milwaukee Braves and other clubs, is one of many happy endings Smalling has encountered. After years of being unable to contact Covington, Smalling discovered that the ex-Brave had moved to Canada. His current address is in the newest edition of the list. "The only impossible players to find," Smalling adds, "are those living outside the United States or Canada. Where they don't speak our language, it's very difficult."

Just how does Smalling find all these current and former players, as well as their home addresses? "Everywhere," Smalling says. "You've really got to dig, but the addresses can be found. It's like the work of an investigative reporter." A few of Smalling's sources for home addresses include phone books from around the country, libraries, high school and college alumni departments and athletic directors, city halls and police departments. He mentions that three men from his hometown went on to play in the National Basketball Association. "I bet that if you called the high school here today, someone there would know how to get in touch with these guys."

One additional source for addresses Smalling named was a state's department of motor vehicles. This method helped him locate former Chicago Cubs star Ernie Banks in California. "If you know the guy's name and his date of birth, you can write to his current state of residence and get his new address," Smalling says. "Then, they'll (the state) write back and tell you what his driver's license number is, and it costs you a dollar. For another dollar, you can send back for his driving record, which has his address on it. That's how I found Ernie Banks. I've located quite a few players that way."

Smalling says that he writes to 5,000 players each year by postcard in an attempt to sell them the book.

Many players, including Ernie Banks, have bought copies. "A lot of them are glad to get it and find out where their old teammates are," Smalling says.

But more than book sales comes from the postcard solicitations. Smalling adds "address correction requested" on each of the postcards. By adding that sentence, the U.S. Postal Service will provide current addresses (if available) for relocated players. "I probably got 200–300 address corrections in one year, and found that six or seven of the players had died," Smalling says. "I got some valuable information for my book, and sold enough copies to pay for my postage."

Yes, a few current and former players have objected to Smalling's book, claiming that it's an invasion of privacy. Recently, former Indians outfielder Rocky Colavito blasted the book in an interview published in *Sports Collectors Digest*. Colavito said that he would not sign fan mail requests if the envelope had been addressed with the home address contained in Smalling's book. Colavito even threatened to take legal action against Smalling for printing his address.

Smalling prefers not to discuss such minor obstacles (a few of which have been in the form of wives of current players objecting to mail at home). In his defense, Smalling says, "Their address, by and large, is public record. There really aren't that many copies of my book published. Besides, they are only one player listed among thousands of names."

Among those names, most have positive reactions to Smalling's directory. Smalling says that some ex-players will send him change of address cards when they move, so he will include their current address in his newest book. One of his favorite examples is Joe Abreu, who played only nine games for the 1942 Cincinnati Reds. "I sent for his autograph, and his address popped up in my book. I wrote him again five years later. He wrote back and told me, 'Since you first got my name and address, and you wrote your book, I've gotten about 400 more autograph requests since then.'"

Smalling's constant research extends past the lives of the players listed. In his address list, he includes the date and location of a player's death when known. He says the information helps collectors determine auto-graph values, since the availability of autographs from deceased players would decrease, naturally.

One bit of advice Smalling has for all collectors is to get autographs from players *before* they become famous. "The key, if you really want to get their autographs, is to go to the minor leagues. I've got some Dwight Gooden au-tographs (from his minor league career). He's not signing for small people now. He's signing for people who want to pay him big bucks. That's ridiculous." Smalling's quick-ness in getting signatures even surprises some players. He says that he'll send baseball cards to many rookies to get autographed. Because the cards are still new, some young players will write him and ask if he'll send them more cards of themselves.

The Baseball Address List is available directly from Smalling for $12.95 shipped by United Parcel Service or $13.70 by first-class mail. Contact Jack Smalling at 2308 Van Buren, Ames, Iowa 50010.

Avid hobbyists may want to ask for their book to be autographed. After all, if autograph collectors were major leaguers, Jack Smalling would be a Hall of Famer. Thanks to his efforts, collectors anywhere have the op-portunity to enjoy this hobby.

When Home Addresses Fail

6

Yes, *The Baseball Address List* is a valuable tool for obtaining home addresses of both current and former players.

However, writing to baseball personalities at their home addresses won't always be a sure-fire success. At times, a home address may be the *worst* source to use in contacting current players.

Frankly, your luck just depends on the attitude of the player you write to. Many men on today's baseball teams feel that signing autographs is a part of their jobs. Therefore, these athletes want to leave their job-related tasks like autograph signing at the ballpark. Players like John Wathan, Dan Quisenberry and Gary Carter are dependable by-mail signers. Mail sent to their homes, though, gets ignored. Writing to Carter in care of the Mets or Wathan in care of the Royals baseball teams would nearly guarantee a response. Many current players simply want their public, on-the-field time separate from their private home lives.

Former players sometimes refuse the mail received from fans and aren't shy about saying so. Hall of Famers Harmon Killebrew, Lefty Gomez and Joe DiMaggio, all at various times in the past, have marked at-home mail "return to sender." These men were living at the addresses noted on the envelopes, according to veteran collector Jack Smalling.

Smalling researched the whereabouts of the trio in 1988. He found that local postmasters will, for $1 a name, confirm the current validity of *any* address. Postal officials reaffirmed that the addresses used by collectors to write the four stars were proper and current. These men merely wanted to avoid the bother of mail. After all, no person is legally required to accept any piece of mail.

It does happen. A couple of years ago, I was scolded by the Phillies front office when I published the home addresses of then-pitcher Larry Andersen and pitching coach Claude Osteen. Team public relations director Vince Nauss told me that many team members felt at-home mail was an invasion of privacy, and these players would often throw away fan mail received at home. However, Nauss added that almost all team members were happy to answer fan mail sent in care of their team.

This doesn't mean that home addresses are bad options. Quite often, they're good ways to reach a former player quickly. Then again, I wouldn't want to write to a member of the Chicago Cubs at his Florida home in May. That player might not return home until October to see any of that mail. By writing to him in care of the Cubs at the Wrigley Field address, the chances are better that my hero would see my letter more quickly.

On the other hand, home addresses will work best during the winter. Current players don't live at the stadium during the winter months. Instead, they'll be spread out across the country living ordinary lives. Many teams even publicly state that they won't forward fan mail during the off-season, but will hold it until the player reports the next spring.

Don't be scared of the skeptics who claim that team addresses *never* work. Some teams will help major stars sort their mail during the season, so the chore of answering 300 letters a week isn't a nightmare. Some players simply will sign the items sent by fans, and player assistants will do the mailing. In the winter, that player may be on his own, answering a summer's buildup of letters. Which situation do you want your letter to fall into?

Some teams—namely the Mets, Royals and Yankees—have, in the past, deserved the criticisms fans have leveled against them for poor distribution of fan mail to players. Many of these teams now provide postcard-sized photos for the players to send to their fans upon request. This trend has proved a boon for fans of other sports, as many football, basketball and hockey players, who often are used to getting a smaller flow of fan mail than their baseball counterparts, will now go to the personal expense of obtaining their own photos to send out to fans.

Despite good mail delivery by most teams, even advanced collectors get overly suspicious of sending fan mail in care of clubs. They feel that letters to players should be sent to home addresses to "beat the rush." That is, some hobbyists believe the notion that megastars and sometimes-signers like Pete Rose or Don Mattingly get little at-home mail and these letters will receive personal care.

Wrong! If a player steadfastly refuses to give autographs, this Scrooge-like behavior is employed with *all* mail. For years, Rose has permitted a husband-and-wife team from Indiana to answer his mail. Fans receive either forgeries or rubber-stamped facsimiles, although the signatures look close to authentic. This secret slipped out when the couple got permission from Rose to market past fan letters in a book. In Mattingly's case, mail sent to the Yankees or to Mattingly's Indiana home was forwarded to a fan club. A fan club application and nothing else would be returned in the fan's self-addressed, stamped envelope. In both cases, use of home or stadium addresses netted the same results.

Former Minnesota Twins slugger Killebrew, a Hall of Fame member, refused all mail in the past. I asked him if he was upset with letters being sent to his home only. "It doesn't matter," he said. "There's too much. Some people write me at home, others write me in care of the Twins, the Baseball Hall of Fame (which forwards mail, too) or WCCO (the radio station where he works broadcasting Twins games)." Later, Killebrew altered his policy and decided to sign one autograph per written request. But previously, he treated *all* mail the same.

The Killebrew episode also shows how a little research can uncover the many ways sports stars can be reached. Various collector publications exist which report success stories of how collectors have reached sports figures using certain addresses. However, daring hobbyists may want to break out on their own and gain their own sources.

Best of all, almost all of these ideas are free. Don't be persuaded by hobby advertisements which offer all baseball team addresses for $3 or the home address of your favorite player for 50 cents. There are alternatives.

For instance, when writing to a sports celebrity, write "address correction requested" below your return address on the envelope the letter is mailed in. If your letter gets returned because the person has moved, a new address may be noted on the envelope (if the person has notified the post office of their new home). It won't always do the trick, but it's a possibility.

If a home address can't be found, find out if the famous person is still associated with a pro team. Team media guides will carry in-depth listings of scouts, minor league coaches, front-office personnel and other workers. Keep an eye out for the names of former players. Then, just note "please forward" on the envelope you mail to the person's current employer, the team.

Does this person broadcast for a radio or TV station now? Lots of ex-jocks do sports reporting. The addresses can be unearthed in metropolitan phone books found at nearly any decent-sized public or college library.

Sometimes, no sports connections can be found for former athletes. But the retirees may cash in on their fame by opening private businesses (restaurants, insurance agencies and more) in their hometowns or the locations where they played. Often, the players will place their names above the title of their businesses, so addresses are easily discovered.

Again, ex-participants of major sports will be easiest to track down. Because no home address lists exist for sports like football, boxing, hockey or basketball, bigger challenges are ahead for collectors.

However, library reference books like Who's Who in America (which is published in regional editions, too) and Current Biography may help. Short profiles of the noted celebrities are published, along with a business address. Tennis players, Olympians, foreign sports

NAME	ADDRESS USED	DATE MAILED	ITEMS SENT	DATE OF RESPONSE	ITEMS RETURNED

stars and members of more obscure teams may be contacted through these resources.

As noted, when hunting autographs, it is possible to stay one move ahead of casual collectors. Don't wait until an athlete gains immortality before seeking an autograph. College athletes can be written to in care of the athletic departments at their schools. Other institutions willing to forward mail to stars are several sports halls of fame. It might be tough to guess the whereabouts of a retired football great like Red Grange. The surest answer is to address Grange's letter in care of the Pro Football Hall of Fame in Canton, Ohio.

Often, the halls will sell reasonably-priced, attractive collectibles like photos or posters, which are great pieces to get autographed. Send a letter to any hall's merchandise department and request a mail-order souvenir list to check out the many possibilities.

The following is a starter list of addresses available for teams in the NFL, NBA and Major League Baseball. For additional addresses, consult the *Comprehensive Directory of Sports Addresses III* by Ed Kobak, Jr.

NATIONAL FOOTBALL LEAGUE

Buffalo Bills, One Bills Dr., Orchard Park, NY 14127

Cincinnati Bengals, 200 Riverfront Stadium, Cincinnati, OH 45202

Cleveland Browns, Tower B, Cleveland Stadium, Cleveland, OH 44114

Denver Broncos, 5700 Logan St., Denver, CO 80216

Houston Oilers, 6910 Fannin St., Houston, TX 77030

Indianapolis Colts, P.O. Box 24100, Indianapolis, IN 46224-0100

Kansas City Chiefs, One Arrowhead Dr., Kansas City, MO 64129

Los Angeles Raiders, 332 Center St., El Segundo, CA 90245

Miami Dolphins, 4700 Biscayne Blvd., Suite 1440, Miami, FL 33137

New England Patriots, Sullivan Stadium, Route 1, Foxboro, MA 02035

New York Jets, 598 Madison Ave., New York, NY 10022

Pittsburgh Steelers, Three Rivers Stadium, 300 Stadium Circle, Pittsburgh, PA 15212

San Diego Chargers, San Diego-Jack Murphy Stadium, P.O. Box 20666, San Diego, CA 92120

Seattle Seahawks, 11220 NE 53rd St., Kirkland, WA 98033

Atlanta Falcons, Suwanee Rd. at I-85, Suwanee, GA 30174

Chicago Bears, Halas Hall, 250 N. Washington, Lake Forest, IL 60045

Dallas Cowboys, Cowboys Center, 1 Cowboys Parkway, Irving, TX 75063-4727

Detroit Lions, Pontiac Silverdome, 1200 Featherstone Rd., Box 4200, Pontiac, MI 48057

Green Bay Packers, 1265 Lombardi Ave., Green Bay, WI 54303

Los Angeles Rams, 2327 W. Lincoln Ave., Anaheim, CA 92801

Minnesota Vikings, 9520 Viking Dr., Eden Prairie, MN 55344

New Orleans Saints, 6928 Saints Ave., Metairie, LA 70003

New York Giants, Giants Stadium, East Rutherford, NJ 07073

Philadelphia Eagles, Veterans Stadium, Broad

Street and Pattison Avenue, Philadelphia, PA 19148

San Francisco 49ers, 711 Nevada St., Redwood City, CA 94061

Tampa Bay Buccaneers, One Buccaneer Place, Tampa, FL 33607

Washington Redskins, P.O. Box 17247, Dulles International Airport, Washington, D.C. 20041

Phoenix Cardinals, P.O. Box 888, Phoenix, AZ 85001

NATIONAL BASKETBALL ASSOCIATION

Atlanta Hawks, 100 Techwood Dr. NW, Atlanta, GA 30303

Boston Celtics, 150 Causeway St., Boston, MA 02114

Chicago Bulls, One Magnificent Mile, 980 N. Michigan Ave., Suite 1600, Chicago, IL 60611

Cleveland Cavaliers, P.O. Box 5000, Richfield, OH 44286

Dallas Mavericks, Reunion Arena, 777 Sports St., Dallas, TX 75207

Denver Nuggets, P.O. Box 4658, Denver, CO 80204-0658

Detroit Pistons, Pontiac Silverdome, 1200 Featherstone Rd., Pontiac, MI 48057

Golden State Warriors, Oakland Coliseum Arena, Oakland, CA 94621

Houston Rockets, The Summit, Houston, TX 77046

Indiana Pacers, Two W. Washington, Suite 510, Indianapolis, IN 46204

Los Angeles Clippers, LA Sports Arena, 3939 S. Figueroa, Los Angeles, CA 90037

Los Angeles Lakers, P.O. Box 10, Inglewood, CA 90306

Milwaukee Bucks, 901 N. Fourth St., Milwaukee, WI 53203

New Jersey Nets, Brendan Byrne Arena, East Rutherford, NJ 07073

New York Knicks, 4 Pennsylvania Plaza, New York, NY 10001

Philadelphia 76ers, Veterans Stadium, P.O. Box 25040, Philadelphia, PA 19147

Portland Trailblazers, 700 NE Multnomah St., Suite 950, Lloyd Building, Portland, OR 97232

Sacramento Kings, 1515 Sports St., Sacramento, CA 95834

San Antonio Spurs, 600 E. Market, Suite 102, San Antonio, TX 78205

Seattle Supersonics, Box C-900911, Seattle, WA 98109-9711

Utah Jazz, 5 Triad Center, 5th Floor, Salt Lake City, UT 84180

Washington Bullets, One Harry S. Truman Dr., Landover, MD 20785

Charlotte Hornets, 2 First Union Plaza, Suite 2600, Charlotte, NC 28282

Miami Heat, Miami Arena, Miami, FL 33136-4102

Orlando Magic, Suite 275, 1 Dupont Center, 390 N. Orange Ave., Orlando, FL 32801

Minnesota Timberwolves, 730 Hennepin Ave., Suite 500, Minneapolis, MN 55403

(note: Minnesota and Orlando join the league for 1989-90.)

MAJOR LEAGUE BASEBALL

Baltimore Orioles, Memorial Stadium, Baltimore, MD 21218

Boston Red Sox, Fenway Park, Boston, MA 02215

California Angels, P.O. Box 2000, Anaheim, CA 92803

Chicago White Sox, Comiskey Park, 324 W. 35th St., Chicago, IL 60616

Cleveland Indians, Municipal Stadium, Cleveland, OH 44114

Detroit Tigers, Tiger Stadium, Detroit, MI 48216

Kansas City Royals, Royals Stadium, Box 1969, Kansas City, MO 64141

Milwaukee Brewers, County Stadium, Milwaukee, WI 53214

Minnesota Twins, The Metrodome, 501 Chicago Ave., South, Minneapolis, MN 55415

New York Yankees, Yankee Stadium, Bronx, NY 10451

Oakland A's, Oakland-Alameda County Coliseum, Oakland, CA 94621

Seattle Mariners, P.O. Box 4100, The Kingdome, Seattle, WA 98104

Texas Rangers, P.O. Box 1111, Arlington Stadium, Arlington, TX 76010

Toronto Blue Jays, Exhibition Stadium, P.O. Box 7777, Adelaide Street Post Office, Toronto, Ontario, Canada M5C 2K7

Atlanta Braves, P.O. Box 4064, Atlanta, GA 30312

Cincinnati Reds, 100 Riverfront Stadium, Cincinnati, OH 45202

Chicago Cubs, Wrigley Field, 1060 W. Addison St., Chicago, IL 60613

Houston Astros, P.O. Box 288, The Astrodome, Houston, TX 77001

Los Angeles Dodgers, Dodger Stadium, 1000 Elysian Park Avenue, Los Angeles, CA 90012

Montreal Expos, P.O. Box 500, Station M, Montreal, Quebec, Canada H1V 3P2

New York Mets, Shea Stadium, Flushing, NY 11368

Philadelphia Phillies, Veterans Stadium, P.O. Box 7575, Philadelphia, PA 19101

Pittsburgh Pirates, P.O. Box 7000, Pittsburgh, PA
   15212
St. Louis Cardinals, Busch Stadium, 250 Stadium
   Plaza, St. Louis, MO 63102
San Diego Padres, Jack Murphy Stadium, 9449 Fri-
   ars Rd., San Diego, CA 92108
San Francisco Giants, Candlestick Park, San Fran-
   cisco, CA 94124

The following are the three major sports hall of
fames in America. All agree to forward mail to members, so mark your letters "please forward."

Baseball Hall of Fame, Box 590, Cooperstown,
   NY 13326
Pro Football Hall of Fame, 2121 George Halas Drive
   NW, Canton, Ohio 44708
Naismith Memorial Basketball Hall of Fame, 1150
   W. Columbus Ave., Springfield, MA 01101

For more information about other specific halls of
fame which might forward mail to members, send
your questions and a legal-size self-addressed,
stamped envelope to the Association of Sports Museums and Halls of Fame, 2141 W. Adams, Los Angeles,
CA 90018.

Getting the Immortals: Collecting the Signatures of Baseball Hall of Famers

7

U ndoubtedly, the most popular autographs among sports fans have to be those signed by members of the Baseball Hall of Fame.

At card shows, you may see big spenders shelling out wads of hundred dollar bills to gain signatures of such deceased legends as Babe Ruth and Lou Gehrig. Both of these Yankee stars enjoyed much fan recognition during their playing days, so they both signed many autographs. Gehrig was a bit more reclusive than Ruth, and he died earlier than the Babe, so the first baseman's signature isn't as plentiful as Ruth's is.

Of course, some other Hall of Famers who were elected posthumously may have signed precious few autographs during their careers. Edd Roush was the Hall's oldest living member at 94 years before he died in 1988. Roush claims that few fans ever cared about autographs before Babe Ruth became famous.

Ruth has been dead for more than 40 years now, but 56 members of the Hall of Fame were living in 1988, following the latest induction ceremonies in Cooperstown, New York. Sadly, nearly half of the living inductees now request some sort of financial compensation before signing a single autograph. The good news, though, is that all but three Hall members were physically able and willing to sign autographs throughout most of 1988.

It's still possible to acquire some in-person signatures during the weekend induction ceremonies (usually the last week in July) at the Baseball Hall of Fame in Cooperstown, although the chances of in-person contact have dwindled considerably in the last 10 years. At the request of members, the Hall of Fame provides an outside security staff to keep the peace among the autograph seekers and the inductees.

In return for increased security, the Hall convinces many members to participate in organized signing sessions each day. The sessions are held at the local Otesaga Hotel, where inductees stay. Hall of Famers (HOFers) provide one free autograph per person in line, but the sessions are usually limited to around one hour. Therefore, many people get shut out. Also, the participating inductees split into two groups to serve a larger number of collectors. The drawback here is that a collector may need to decide at the last minute what signatures are the most desirable. Eddie Mathews and Hank Aaron may be sitting at one table, while Ted Williams and Bobby Doerr may be at another.

In 1988, 26 different Hall members participated in at least one of the sessions. Even members like Roy Campanella or Negro League star James "Cool Papa" Bell, who cannot sign due to health problems, still sit in on the sessions and greet fans as they pass by.

Because the number of collectors able to participate in each session is limited, it's advisable to line up early in the morning to reserve a spot. Fortunately, one of the three sessions is reserved exclusively for fans ages 15 and under.

These sessions take considerable time and expense for the Hall of Fame to provide, but the Hall wants to let the public participate in the festivities. Ted Spencer, Hall curator, and Tom Heitz, Hall librarian, help oversee all the sessions. As Hall officials, both men get lots of unwarranted criticisms from collectors who want to break the rules. "They want multiple autographs or signatures only from certain individuals," Spencer says. "We had a few problems in 1988. The sessions are designed so people can get up to a dozen autographs free. If you tried to get these signatures at a hobby show, you'd pay $10 to $15 apiece." Spencer says that everyone at the Hall puts considerable effort into producing these public events, so it's understandably frustrating when "hate mail" comes from someone who felt cheated by the sessions.

Heitz agrees. "The weekend activities are designed for the members," he says. "It's their weekend."

Spencer admits that the lack of appreciation from the public has tempted the Hall administration to scrap the signing sessions entirely. Such a decision would be understandable, but the lost opportunities would be a hobby tragedy. To help collectors know what to expect, Spencer and Heitz both are willing to answer questions by mail to better outline the rules for the sessions. Write either man at the address which follows. Enclose a self-addressed, stamped envelope for a quicker reply.

Getting in-person autographs in Cooperstown is obviously thrilling, but can be hit-and-miss. The Hall members hang around the hotel, and don't normally stroll the streets of Cooperstown signing for one and all.

A more costly but dependable alternative is attending a hobby show. Nearly all living HOF members have appeared at card shows on a regular basis. In many cases, Joe DiMaggio, Ted Williams and Mickey Mantle signatures will cost $20 each, but this is the only guaranteed way of getting this superstar trio to sign anything.

Newer collectors who are unsure if they want to invest this amount in the autographs of some HOFers can succeed in getting the signatures of other amiable Hall members by mail. It's possible to reach any Hall of Fame member by mail in care of the Baseball Hall of Fame, Box 590, Cooperstown, NY 13326. Be sure to mark your letter "personal, please forward." Granted, home addresses can be found in *The Baseball Address List*, but budget-minded collectors can use the same address to contact *all* Hall members.

Starting with some of the most willing signers, here's a member-by-member rundown on the signing habits of the HOFers:

BROOKS ROBINSON—He'd have to get my vote for best-known, most willing signer of baseball's living legends. True, Robinson does appear at card shows (the right to get his autograph will be hawked at anywhere from $3 to $7 per signature by promoters). However, Robinson usually signs all by-mail requests sent to him within two weeks, using his trademark looping penmanship.

During his career, Robinson would send out extra team photos of himself upon request. Often, he now sends out the notable brown-gold Hall of Fame plaque postcard of himself. (Request a postcard when writing to any member. The Hall will furnish them free to members upon request so they can use them to answer fan mail with.) Don't judge him too harshly if he takes up to a month during the season to respond, because his travels as a team broadcaster make regular mail delivery tough. Still, "Brooks Robby" is a true friend both for fans and hobbyists.

CHARLIE GEHRINGER—His autograph (signed "Chas.") is bold and precise. Back when everyone exclusively used ball-point pens for signing, Gehringer's confident strokes would literally chisel his name on paper. Gehringer remains a great by-mail signer, taking only a couple of weeks tops.

STAN MUSIAL—"Stan the Man" has done an increased number of hobby show appearances. Thankfully, Musial hasn't taken the lead of other HOF show guests who don't sign by mail simply to increase the demand from autograph collectors. The former Cardinal is a prompt and reliable autograph signer.

LOU BOUDREAU—Best remembered as the playing manager for the Cleveland Indians, Boudreau is a slow but consistent signer. Be sure to request all your items to be signed on the *front* because Boudreau previously tended to autograph postcards and baseball cards on their back sides. Boudreau is also reachable in care of the Chicago Cubs, where he still serves as a team broadcaster.

BOBBY DOERR—This former Red Sox infielder always signs his name "Bob" to save time. He is one of the quickest respondents in the Hall today.

RICK FERRELL—Due to Ferrell's advanced age, he sometimes takes six months to one year to respond. However, patient collectors can get his signature by mail.

LEFTY GOMEZ—"El Goofo" is on again, off again, in his mail replies. In the past, he's refused fan mail sent to his house, so it comes back unopened.

Gomez does do several card show appearances, too, so valuable items might be safest when signed via the show circuit.

BILLY HERMAN—One of the vintage, lesser-known Hall members, Herman is fast and prompt in his replies to fan mail. Herman also appears at card shows, so his autographs are widely available.

A.B. "HAPPY" CHANDLER—This was the baseball commissioner who opened the door for Jackie Robinson to break baseball's color barrier. However, because he wasn't an actual player, many show promoters neglect Chandler as a show guest. Although he isn't fast in his replies, he will respond by mail. He enclosed two different photos of himself with my last letter, although I had requested only one signature on an index card.

GEORGE KELL—Younger fans may know Kell as a Tigers announcer, instead of as a quality infielder. Kell is a quick signer, although he responds quickest in the off-season (when he isn't traveling with the team).

BOB LEMON—He's quick, too! "Lem" signs in ballpoint pen, so you may want to send him a Sharpie to use if you want his autograph in another type of ink.

ENOS SLAUGHTER—The man nicknamed "Country" is back on his farm after a long career in the majors. He is a quick signer by mail and is inexpensive to obtain in-person at card shows. Slaughter waited many years to gain Hall of Fame induction from the Veteran's Committee. Now, he constantly proves his worth as a HOFer by displaying a championship attitude toward collectors.

DUKE SNIDER—Don't try to get Snider's autograph during the summer, because he's busy broadcast-

ROBERT WILLIAM ANDREW FELLER

CLEVELAND A.L. 1936 TO 1941
1945 TO 1956
PITCHED 3 NO-HIT GAMES IN A.L.,12 ONE HIT
GAMES, SET MODERN STRIKEOUT RECORD
WITH 18 IN GAME, 348 FOR SEASON, LED
A.L. IN VICTORIES 6 (ONE TIE) SEASONS,
LIFE TIME RECORD: WON 266, LOST 162,
P.C.,621, E.R. AVERAGE 3.25, STRUCKOUT 2581.

NATIONAL BASEBALL HALL OF FAME & MUSEUM
Cooperstown, New York

An inexpensive, popular collectible is the set of postcards issued by the Baseball Hall of Fame. The postcards, which cost only 25 cents apiece, show the plaque of each HOF member.

ing games for the Montreal Expos. In the winter, however, Snider is a sure-fire reply by mail. He appears at many card shows, also.

ED STACK—Who's he? The president of the Baseball Hall of Fame, of course. Stack is pictured on a Perez-Steele art postcard, even though he never played Major League Baseball. Anyone wanting a "complete" Hall of Fame collection should contact Stack, too, for he signs willingly.

JOHNNY MIZE—"The Big Cat" asks for a tiny donation of $1 per signature, with checks made payable to one of two deserving organizations in his hometown:

A personal note from Bob Feller makes this signature even more special than his signed Hall of Fame card.

The Demoresɪ (Ga.) Boy Scouts, or the Demorest Women's Club. Mize attends lots of card shows, too, but he'll be more expensive there.

JOCKO CONLAN—Jocko is the only living umpire belonging to the Hall of Fame. Jocko, as he nears age 90, signs only some fan mail requests. Fans who send him offbeat letters, such as notes about today's umpires handling temperamental managers, may get short letters in return. Jocko is unpredictable.

JOE SEWELL—Sewell requests a $2 payment for each autograph, but will respond quickly when a payment is enclosed.

ROBIN ROBERTS—A veteran college baseball coach in Florida, Roberts requests a $2 donation per signature, made payable to the USF baseball program. He uses the proceeds to fund scholarship programs.

ED MATHEWS—This power-hitting third baseman charges $1 per autograph. He appears at many card shows, but the fees are much higher there.

AL LOPEZ—Lopez appears at a few card shows. He often returns fans' items back blank. If he does sign an autograph, he'll only sign one.

RALPH KINER—The Mets broadcaster is slow responding to fan mail. He wants donations for all signatures, $3 for flat items and $5 for baseballs, made payable to Kenneth Copeland Ministries.

BOB FELLER—Feller bragged to a hobby writer once that he "had signed more autographs than anyone in history." Feller undoubtedly has made more hobby show appearances than any other living Hall of Famer. However, he always earns his money by shaking hands, greeting fans and offering to personalize all items. Feller and his wife keep track of fan letters received. Admirably, he will sign one autograph free for a fan, but will charge $3 per each additional signature request.

DON DRYSDALE—Drysdale once was a willing signer. The abundance of autograph dealers cashing in on his generosity convinced him to quit dispensing free signatures. Now, he asks for $3 per signature in the form of a money order.

YOGI BERRA—Collectors do the best writing Berra in care of the Astros, where he is a coach. Try contacting him there during the season.

RAY DANDRIDGE—A former Negro League star, Dandridge is retired, and supports himself and his wife by revenue he generates signing autographs. He requests $3 per signature (for a flat item), or $10 to sign a Perez-Steele postcard of himself. Dandridge appears at several card shows.

JIM "CATFISH" HUNTER—Hunter tries to sign his fan mail only once or twice a year to discourage large volumes of letters. He plays at a few old-timer's games and appears at some card shows.

BILLY WILLIAMS—Williams is doing more and more card shows each year. Because of his travel schedule and his work as a Chicago Cubs coach, he doesn't answer his mail for months at a time.

HARMON KILLEBREW—Killebrew claimed in a recent interview with writer Pete Dobrovitz in *Sports Collectors Digest*, "You'll just have to write to me and take your chances." Previously, Killebrew had refused fan mail sent to him, and then he decided to sign one autograph for free and charge $4 for additional ones. Killebrew appears at many card shows during the off-season when he isn't announcing for the Twins. However, his attitude towards fan mail changes regularly. Good luck.

AL KALINE—Kaline signs only a few fan mail requests. Autograph veteran Dave Miedema recently observed in one hobby column he wrote that Kaline primarily answers letters from children and women. The best bet is to find him at a card show.

SANDY KOUFAX—Koufax has erratic signing

habits through the mail. If you do write to him, do contact him in care of the Hall. Don't risk sending any valuable items.

MONTE IRVIN—Previously, he has charged $2 per signature. Donations can be made either to the United Negro College Fund or St. Mary's Hospital.

WARREN SPAHN—Spahn sometimes skips the signing sessions during the Hall of Fame inductions so he can play golf in Cooperstown. Don't expect him to sign fan mail quickly or to sign more than one item. Spahn can be found at many card shows throughout the year.

Sadly, Bill Terry, Buck Leonard and "Cool Papa" Bell aren't physically able to respond to autograph requests. I'm sure, though, that they'd appreciate kind notes from fans who simply would send their best wishes.

How can you get the other living Hall of Famers by mail? Basically, you can't. Of course, you are free to try, but your chances of getting a free autograph by mail aren't much better than winning a state lottery. Most of the time, fans can kiss their collectibles goodbye when writing to the following players:

Willie Mays, Hank Aaron, Willie Stargell, Mickey Mantle, Whitey Ford, Joe DiMaggio, Ted Williams, Bob Gibson, Luis Aparicio and Juan Marichal (both live outside the United States, and are difficult to *locate* by mail), Ernie Banks, Hoyt Wilhelm, Frank Robinson, Pee Wee Reese, Willie McCovey, Bill Dickey, Early Wynn, Lou Brock and Luke Appling.

Smart fans will start reaching tomorrow's Hall of Famers *today*. It's cheaper than playing the stock market, and a lot more fun. Remember, people like Dickey, Reese and Appling once freely answered fan mail. But their sudden superstardom that came with their Hall of Fame election brought floods of mail. This, combined with the shady commercial practices of some hobby dealers, pushed these ex-players into marketing their own signatures.

When the Hall of Fame balloting is released each spring, look at the vote totals. Tony Oliva, Jim Bunning and Orlando Cepeda are three contenders who have made many top 10 appearances in the voting. Also, read some baseball history books. Diehard fans will be happy to give their opinions on overlooked celebrities from baseball's past. Leo Durocher, Dick Bartell, and Negro Leaguer Lou Dials are but a few names of possibles who could be inducted in the future by the Hall of Fame Veteran's Committee.

One of the biggest thrills a retired player can have is a sincere compliment from a fan who'd recommend that athlete for the Baseball Hall of Fame.

So don't wait until these players are formally inducted to the Hall. When this happens, you'll be competing with thousands of other collectors who want the same signatures you do. Start a Hall of Fame in your own autograph collection and beat Cooperstown to the punch.

How to Hunt Down Autograph Possibilities

8

M ost newcomers in the sports autograph hobby want to get sig-
natures only from the greatest stars of today. This might
seem like an awesome challenge, due to the fact that
thousands of other fans may want autographs from the
very same stars.

However, true stars seldom fade from the public's
eye, even after they retire from sports. Many get
chances at television or radio announcing. Other ex-
athletes do commercials or get involved in acting. Others stay in their respective sports as referees, coaches or
front-office executives. In any case, many opportunities
remain for obtaining autographs from these celebrities,
years after retirement.

But what about the lesser-known names in sports
history? Rookies who never won a spot on a team's roster or future legends with careers snuffed out by inju-
ries are only two types of players who almost evaporate
from society once they leave sports. These forgotten
people may be willing autograph signers, but few people
know where they are located.

This classic enigma faces collectors pursuing auto-

Sometimes the most interesting autographs don't come from superstars. Shown are two 1976 Topps cards. Harry Rasmussen legally changed his first name to Eric later in his career, which explains the two different signatures.

graphs on entire sets of baseball cards. It seems that each year, out of 600 to 800 cards made for any given set, a few of the cards will feature players who never made it to their parent team's big-league roster. *The Baseball Address List*, that noted directory of home addresses for former major leaguers, can't help here. What results is that the few collectors who are able to locate these obscure players have a hobby bonanza. These lucky hobbyists do well trading even the home addresses of these unknowns to other anxious collectors.

How's it done? There's really no magic involved. It just takes some patience and a few trips to your nearest public or school library. Start with the last information known about the person. Try to dig up the player's only baseball card. Card backs contain vital information on every player depicted, including height, weight, place of birth and hometown.

Chances are that you'll find someone in the player's listed hometown who could help you in your search. Maybe that player moved on a decade ago. Still, you might spot his same last name in a phone book for that community. That person could be a relative who could furnish some vital information. Yes, most libraries have extensive telephone directories free for the using.

Telephone books may lead you directly to the person for whom you're searching. After even a brief career in pro sports, many retired players (even average, unknown names) will open their own business under their own name. Be it "Babe Ruth's Restaurant" or "John Doe's Sporting Goods," you'd be surprised at the number of people who try to cash in on their athletic pasts.

Here's another idea: It's likely that this mystery athlete is still well-known at his high school or college. Try calling or writing the athletic department where he played, and ask about his current whereabouts.

Occasional clues will pop up in newspapers and magazines, which can be found at your library. While your local newspaper might ignore news on former Mets or Yankees baseball players, New York area publications might offer many "where are they now?" types of features. Of course, when a mention is made of a former player's current occupation, there won't be an address included. That mystery is for you to solve.

An ambitious autograph hound could become a hobby hero by hunting down the current whereabouts of many former football, basketball or hockey players. Collector Jack Smalling's research has allowed hobbyists by-mail access to virtually any living member of major league baseball. If fans had the same reference guide with which to contact retired players from other sports, autograph collecting would be revolutionized.

Take some time to discover the many resources your library offers. Make friends with the reference desk staff, and tell them your aims. The librarians may have additional suggestions for you.

One additional suggestion is to try researching the autograph possibilities in other professional sports. Billiards, bowling, boxing or any other sport—they are all honored with special museums and hall of fames.

An earlier chapter discussed how the baseball, football or basketball hall of fames would forward mail to their respective members. What about a smaller sport? How would these other halls respond?

It depends. Some of these organizations have large staffs and budgets and can afford to assist fans. Other so-called hall of fames may actually be no more than small, informal two-person operations.

Just like the major halls, some of these organizations plan yearly events for all their inductees (creating a field day for collectors). Some halls may sell photos and publications telling about their sports and their members. New collectors should try contacting some celebrities from sports like rodeo or swimming just to compare their responses to baseball, football and basketball players. Then it's clear how stars of major sports sometimes ignore fan mail. Overlooked athletes in other sectors are delighted with fan support, and will respond accordingly.

Here are a few addresses for various hall of fames. One library reference book containing more information on various halls is *Encyclopedia of Sports*, published by A.S. Barnes and Company. The addresses include:

Professional Golf Association Hall of Fame, 100 Avenue of Champions, Palm Beach Gardens, FL 33410

Professional Pool Players Association Hall of Fame, 422 N. Broad Street, Elizabeth, NJ 07206

Billiards Hall of Fame, P.O. Box 15365, Milwaukee, WI 53215

World Golf Hall of Fame, Gerald Ford Blvd., Pinehurst, NC 28374

National Jockeys Racing Hall of Fame, Pimlico Race Course, Baltimore, MD 21215

National Horse Racing Hall of Fame, Union Ave., Saratoga Springs, NY 12866

Auto Racing Hall of Fame, Indianapolis Motor Speedway, Speedway, IN 46224

U.S. Figure Skating Hall of Fame, 20 First Street, Colorado Springs, CO 80966

Amateur Athletic Foundation and Hall of Fame, 2141 Adams Blvd., Los Angeles, CA 90018

U.S. Hockey Hall of Fame, Hat Trick Ave., Eleveth, MN 55734

International Hockey Hall of Fame, Exhibition Place, Toronto, Ontario M6K 3C3 Canada

Boxing Hall of Fame, The Ring Magazine, 120 West 31st, New York, NY 10001

National Bowling Association Hall of Fame, 377 Park Avenue, New York, NY 10016

Professional Bowlers Association Hall of Fame, 1720 Meriman Road, Akron, OH 44313

National Bowling Museum and Hall of Fame, 111 Stadium Plaza, St. Louis, MO 63102

National Football Foundation and Hall of Fame, King's Island, P.O. Box 300, Kings Mill, OH 45034

These are just a few of the institutions which might serve fans and collectors. If one of these organizations has a museum close to you, try to arrange a visit. Virtually all sports museums display some autographed artifacts, signed by the athletes who made the items famous. Some halls for major sports like baseball have research libraries, which can be helpful in authenticating old signatures in some cases. Visiting these locales can be the best way to view rare autographs up close.

The Challengers: How to Cope with Stingy Signers

9

S adly, few (if any) collectors will ever be able to get autographs from every sports personality they approach. That's a sobering fact of life for new hobbyists.

Why would any current or former player ever want to deny an admiring fan a simple signature? The typical explanations of large egos or public contempt are relevant sometimes. Other times, though, the reasonings of non-signers are more deep and puzzling.

Take Mike Marshall, one of baseball's finest relief aces of the 1970s. Marshall's reasons for declining autograph requests sound more humble than arrogant. In an article in *Sports Collectors Digest*, Marshall explains his autograph policies to reporter Tot Holmes, saying, "I never did sign and I still don't. The reason is very simple. I'm not important enough for anyone to want my signature. I'm not going to pretend I am. I have nothing against the people who are asking for the autograph. I'm glad to say 'Hi' and shake their hands. Later in my career I started handing out photo postcards. I just can't stand there like someone they should be fawning over. I don't feel like I am that important to them.

"Now I think I was to my daughters and I think I am to the people I teach—to these people I am generating something; I am someone important. But I'm not going to promote a myth that major league baseball players have some value in this society other than entertainment."

Interestingly, later in his career as a member of the Minnesota Twins Marshall supposedly was convinced by a few fans that they wanted his autograph only to complete their set of team autographs. In most cases, fans who'd treat a player so casually would be ignored in return.

Other current and former stars are concerned about their lack of privacy. Jack Smalling's home address list has enraged some baseball players who don't want to be bothered at home. Sadly, many of these reclusive types will throw away all the fan mail they receive. Milwaukee Brewers Cy Young Award winner Pete Vuckovich told me this in hopes that he wouldn't receive other letter requests. Rocky Colavito warned one hobby writer that he might take legal action against Smalling. (People like Colavito don't know that mailing addresses are matters of public information.)

The biggest concern among baseball's membership today is the fear of being victimized financially. Nine out of every 10 players today insist that all of their autographs are being resold after they are given out freely. Unfortunately, a few stars realize that they have no need to sign autographs for nothing at their park or by mail, when hobby show promoters will gladly fork over a few thousand dollars to gain the star's signing abilities as a show guest.

Baseball's big names can't be blamed totally for this approach. Watch how a player who signs one autograph for a fan in person will suddenly attract 50 other fans demanding more of the same. The celebrity quickly gets the idea that disappointing everyone is much faster and easier than pleasing some of the people some of the time. Of course, compromises can be struck to please everyone. Before Joe DiMaggio began raking in incredible appearance fees, he used admirable methods to handle crowds at old-timer's games. He would announce to collectors that he'd sign only one item per person, and that he wanted fans to stand quietly in line to wait for their turn. Also, DiMaggio threatened to stop signing for everyone if he caught someone sneaking back in line for a second autograph.

Other current and former players have found that they can control autograph demand and support charity by requesting donations for signatures. Oakland A's catcher Terry Steinbach has created a college scholarship fund which he subsidizes by charging $1 per autograph, more for personalizations and the signing of larger items like bats or balls. Some ex-players, out of fear that their autographs are instantly resold, will request small payments simply for themselves. In instances like these, a collector's items will be returned safe but unsigned, along with a note explaining the payment needed to acquire autographs.

How can a collector prove to stars that they aren't part-time dealers merely wanting to instantly sell the signatures they get? First of all, *don't* ask, either in person or by mail, to get two or more of the same items to be signed. Why would any collector want to keep two identical photos in one collection? It's easy to guess that the hobbyist will soon be trading or selling the duplicate. When I'd send two of the same card to a certain player, I would often give the second one to my younger brother. However, I'd state this in a letter.

Honesty pays! On many occasions, the athlete would enclose not one, but *two* extra, unrequested signed photos. One would be personalized "To Tom," the other for my brother would say "To Matt."

Speaking of personalizations, don't be afraid to request them. Former Cardinals catcher Darrell Porter learned that he could personalize all the autographs he signed as a way to frustrate would-be dealers. Soon, however, Porter seemed to tire of the extra work and answered only some fan letters. Players like Porter might be pleased with a fan who, as a good-faith gesture to prove that the signatures wouldn't be sold, requested personalizations.

Still, some stars won't budge with any type of collector persuasions. These sports figures will insist on being paid to sign, only in the controlled setting of a hobby show appearance. Don't think that I'm crazy about paying for signatures, because I try to avoid this situation whenever possible. In many cases, though, paying for a signature at a show can be a surprising bargain.

Future Hall of Fame hurler Steve Carlton is a classic example of how hobby shows bring players out of their shells. Carlton steadfastly avoided the press during his career. He was always polite with fans, but constantly declined autograph requests. Now, Carlton seems delighted to appear at several shows a year. For as little as $7, hobby show attendees get to acquire the signature of a charming, amiable superstar. Outside of a show, Carlton remains his shy, elusive self.

To benefit out-of-town hobbyists, most larger shows run ads in the hobby press which offer collectors the chance to buy signatures by mail. An ad will read something like, "Your item—$9 plus SASE." This means that the collectors must send in their own possession to have signed, along with a container for the item's return which has both the collector's address affixed along with sufficient return postage. Maybe the fee for mail-in items will be almost twice as high as fees for in-person autographs. But, after reading the following scenario, you'll see how it can be worth it.

Now suppose I had a scored Wrigley Field scorecard from 1969. Maybe this was a personal memento from a game I attended. Suppose Ernie Banks had belted a game-winning home run in that game, and I had the whole affair documented on my personal scorecard.

Anyone who read the chapter on Hall of Famers' signing habits will know that Banks signs very few fan mail requests he receives. My little scorecard, which has sentimental value no money can replace, could be trashed if I send this to Ernie's home address. Instead, I follow the instructions found in the hobby show ad promoting Banks' next appearance. I may spend $9 plus another $3 in padded envelopes and postage costs. But I'll get my souvenir back signed, safe and sound. How much would I have invested in time and money to travel to that card show to get Banks to sign the item in person?

To help speed along your mail-in items, try affixing peel-off address labels on the backs of your items (just in case other people send in the same items which could get mixed up). Also, read the ads carefully. A few promoters may go to the trouble of getting a short personalization on an item if you request it. Regardless, always specify where your item should be signed and what color and type of ink you want used on the item.

Ambitious show promoters will sell certain items signed by their show guest. Many times, autographed color photos of widely-recognized names will sell for as little as $6 postpaid. Selected baseball cards, Hall of Fame plaque postcards and other goodies may be offered as well at surprisingly reasonable prices. Check out the small print in those ads.

When using any form of collecting, it's important to keep detailed records of your attempts for signatures. This information can be swapped with other collectors. Letter writers benefit most from this system. Whenever I send out a letter to a sports celebrity, I note the following facts on a chart:

1. When was the letter sent out?
2. What address was the letter sent to?
3. How many items were enclosed for signing?

When a response arrives in the mail box, I add the following facts:

1. How long did the response take?
2. Were all my items returned?
3. Were all my items signed?
4. Were the items personalized?
5. Was an extra photo included?

With this information, fellow collectors can tell you not to waste your time and energy (as well as risking the loss of valuable collectibles) by writing to a non-signer. On the other hand, signers are usually gracious to all fans, so the word spreads quickly.

Most collectors who keep these records find that at least 75 percent of retired players sign, compared to around 60 percent for current players.

Remember, it's not always a lost cause with someone who never returns your items you requested to be signed. After three months, I'll send a followup postcard (which saves money) which reads like this:

> Dear _____,
> I am writing to politely remind you about a letter I sent to you on (list the date).
> I realize you must receive hundreds of fan letters each week. Plus, I understand that a person of your fame has countless other responsibilities.
> However, I truly hope that you will be able to autograph the (list the item(s)) I sent to you before. They are from my personal collection, and I'll be proud to have them signed by you. If it's not possible to autograph these at this time, I'll understand if you can return my items unsigned. Because these items are from my collection, I'd hate to lose them.
> Thank you.
>
> Sincerely,
> Tom Owens

This reminder can bring back cards safely, and it can get tardy but well-meaning players to sign. Occasionally, I'll get a note of apology enclosed back with my autographed cards. Never, by all means, threaten someone by mail to sign your items or else. Harsh words never impress anyone.

After all, your fan letter can be treated just like common junk mail. Your words may get into a star's home, but that celebrity has no legal obligation to fulfill your requests.

Using these strategies, and reading up in autograph hobby columns beforehand for tips from other collectors, can help. Autographing habits change like the wind. Some current players get fed up with public adoration and shun autographs. Former stars sometimes miss the limelight and welcome fan support again after ignoring their supporters for years.

So remember, with persistence and patience, even the stubbornest non-signer may be captured in ink someday!

How to Showcase Your Collection

10

Any autograph, no matter how attractive, seems a bit useless crammed in a shoebox or hidden in a dark closet. Creative collectors, however, don't stop imagining once they obtain a signature. For devoted hobbyists, sharing their collection through an attractive display makes their efforts worthwhile.

There is no one proper way to display a collection. The only requirement is that the condition of all signed items is maintained, so that the value of all autographs is maintained.

One of the most popular items for autograph hounds today is the signed photograph. Quite often, these are displayed in a variety of plastic sleeve-like pages which are fitted for three-ring binders. Magnetic page photo albums with sticky backs may transfer the adhesive to your photos.

Plastic sheets are a fine, inexpensive option. However, some precautions should be taken. Celebrities and collectors alike use Sharpie permanent markers to get photos autographed. This marker produces a clear, vibrant signature on any photo. "We recommend it for signing photographs," says Jane Voigt, a marketing assistant for Sanford Corporation, producers of the marker. "The pen's ink was designed for non-porous surfaces, including glass, metal, wood and plastic."

Sharpies are fine tools for autographing photos. But the photos should not be inserted into a plastic sheet while the signature is still wet. When a photo with a wet autograph gets slapped under plastic, the autograph may be sucked directly from the photo onto the plastic page. Permanent damage is caused to the signed photo. Sometimes days or weeks may pass before the damage is apparent. These mishaps cannot be blamed solely on the ink, the photo or the plastic sheet. If the hobbyist would have waited even 24 hours, the chances for disaster would have subsided.

On some glossy finish photos, the Sharpie ink will not immediately absorb into the photo (even though the signature appears normal). Actually, the ink is sitting on top of the surface of the photo, because the glossy finish hasn't absorbed ink quickly. Matte finish photos have duller finishes which are more receptive to signing. Photos signed in ball-point pen don't run this risk, because the signatures almost become engraved in the photo's surface.

Framed photographs should be displayed out of direct sunlight, which will cause fading. Rapid temperature changes and humid areas should be avoided as well. Try to keep photos (or any autographed items) free of staples, masking or transparent tape, rubber cement or other similar adhesives, because in the long run these can cause damage.

Unsigned photographs can dress up ordinary signed index cards or other simple signatures by combining the two elements in one frame. A double-matte

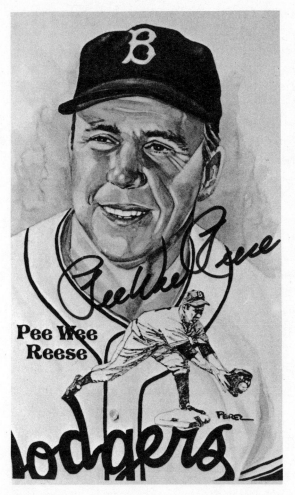

One of the most popular and expensive items collectors want signed today is the limited-edition Perez-Steele art postcard. Only 10,000 of each card are made, and all of them are in private hands. This postcard, authentically signed, might fetch more than $40 today. (copyright Perez-Steele galleries, Fort Washington, Pa.)

can showcase both a photo and a signature (which was obtained separately) under the same glass. Collectors of Perez-Steele Hall of Fame art postcards use this method to display cards of deceased HOFers. Lloyd Waner and Satchel Paige died shortly after their cards were issued, so they had the chance to sign only a few of the P-S cards. An affordable alternative to a signed card is matting a signed index card from either man and placing his P-S card (or other photo) above.

One of the biggest frustrations for collectors of autographed photos is the lack of wall space to display signed treasures. However, if a collector has more shelf space, an autographed baseball collection can be substituted.

Baseballs can be displayed in various protective holders available from hobby dealers and advertisers in hobby periodicals. One new product is called a Ballqube. Unlike most domed, circular plastic holders on the market, the Ballqube is a square, lucite holder. Its shape allows a collector to view all sides of a signed baseball at once. Domed holders cannot offer this advantage.

Again, the best ways to preserve a signed ball are to keep it out of sunlight and away from human hands. Lacquers, varnishes and other protective coatings are sometimes detrimental, causing some balls to yellow prematurely. Others may work, but will harm the ball's appearance if applied in a runny, uneven fashion. My best advice is to get the ball in a specially-designed holder (which should sell for under $3 in most cases). Flamboyant hobbyists will find more expensive autographed ball holders mounted on wooden pedestals, with photo frames, card holders or in other stylish configurations.

Autographed sports cards are popular because of their small size and their availability. However, collectors who acquire hundreds of autographed trading cards will realize soon that they might fill up dozens of protective cardboard boxes or several binders stuffed with plastic sheets.

Try searching through hobby advertisements for several types of plastic and lucite card holders suited for display. These may range from card holders designed like small picture frames to a multi-pocket plastic sheet which could be hung poster style on a wall. In either case, these accessories could allow a collector to display selected favorite autographs for short periods of time, much like revolving exhibitions at an art gallery.

Don't overlook autograph preservation, but don't forget to let a displayed collection reflect your own personality, too. It might be worthwhile to display a short caption explaining how some extra special in-person autographs were acquired. Besides preserving the memories, it would make the autographs more meaningful for others who would learn how hard you worked to get those signatures. References such as "my first autograph" or "obtained in person" displayed by the signature would prove that your collectible had special meaning.

Most of all, a well-done display can convince skeptical friends and relatives that your collecting pursuits aren't trivial. Once they see the impressive array of signatures you've assembled, you may wind up teaching would-be collectors the fundamentals of the hobby. After all, sharing with others is one of the biggest joys of collecting sports autographs.

Value and Authenticity: Autograph Collecting's Two Mysteries

11

"How much is it worth?"
"Is it real or is it fake?"

These questions are bound to puzzle all levels of autograph collectors. The value and authenticity of autographs are complex subjects where easy answers are rare. Only with a little knowledge and a lot of care can collectors be prepared to face these two challenges in the hobby world.

Value. This question comes to mind both when a hobbyist acquires any new signature for a collection or when a desirable autograph is being sold in the open market.

What influences value? Mostly supply and demand. The one aspect which controls supply and demand most in the autograph hobby is death. Any celebrity, no matter how plentiful his or her autograph was during life, will become a higher-demand autograph after death. If a TV western were made about this event, it would be called "Dead Men Sign No Autographs."

Of course, the demand for signatures will vary, depending on the supply of autographs available during the player's life. Noted collector Jack Smalling was once willing to sell autographed index cards of deceased baseball Hall of Famer Stan Coveleski for only $1. Why? He had accumulated more than 600 of them before Coveleski died. Other Hall of Famers, such as Ted Williams, Joe DiMaggio and Mickey Mantle, are valued at much higher levels than lesser-known HOFers. Such immortals always have enjoyed a greater degree of fame (partly because they played in more modern eras). Also, Williams, DiMaggio and Mantle have been much more stingy with their autographs during the last five years. Finding these men appearing at card shows has been the only alternative for autograph collectors wanting signatures, and this option costs at least $15 a crack.

But don't be fooled into thinking that *any* Hall of Fame signature is exceedingly valuable. Antique dealers, some sporting goods shops and other general-interest type businesses will ask double-digit prices for items signed by famous ex-players like Brooks Robinson or Stan Musial. Both men are normally happy to sign autographs by mail, and have done so for years. Any respectable sports memorabilia dealer wouldn't ask more than $10 for an ordinary autographed photo of either man. Unknowing (or unscrupulous) non-hobby merchants may try to get more than three times that rate from uninformed fans. I've seen some shops in Cooperstown try this stunt. Fans unaware of a star's signing habits may think this is a bargain. Think again!

As a general rule, HOFers who played before the 1940s signed fewer autographs, mostly because fewer fans wanted signatures from *anyone*. Therefore, a man like Frank "Home Run" Baker could be a tough autograph simply due to time. Baker played from 1908 through 1922. He was elected to the Hall of Fame in 1955 at the age of 69. He died in 1963 at age 77. Because the autograph collecting hobby didn't gain widespread acceptance until the 1970s, it's unlikely that many hobbyists had the perseverance to secure Baker's signature.

Using a baseball encyclopedia can help beginning collectors determine values by setting up time lines of when a player would have been signing. Lesser-known players like Danny Thompson, Mike Miley, Dan Frisella, Don Wilson or Ken Hubbs may be on the "want lists" of lots of veteran collectors. All five of these men died before their careers were over. Such unnatural events lower the supply and increase the demand for specific autographs.

Of course, the value of an individual signature may depend upon the item which has been signed. Generally, signed photographs (postcard-sized or larger) are most desired and valued the highest by collectors. If a photo has special historical significance (such as Pete Rose celebrating after he broke Ty Cobb's record for hits) the value would increase. Personally, I would look for a signed photo first because of the subject matter and next because photos are easy to display.

More and more hobbyists, however, are collecting autographed baseballs, bats and other equipment. Getting a piece of game-used equipment, signed by the player the piece originated from, seems to validate the authenticity of the item and increase its value. Bats and balls, though, are catching on with larger segments of the hobby most rapidly. Usually, these items see a yearly increase in worth because they are universal symbols of the game of baseball.

Authenticity is a key here again. Concerning bats, try to determine if the bat was actually game-used or was simply modeled after the player's own bat. Bat signatures should be clear and bold, usually from a Sharpie marker.

Balls are a bit more complicated. Value should be based on the number of signatures on the ball, and if the ball has the official American or National League logo (along with a facsimile signature from the league's commissioner). Official league balls will be worth up to 25 percent more than an ordinary baseball. Also, check if the ball has random signatures, or if the ball is from the roster of one team from one specific season. Unless "random" baseballs have some historical meaning (such as a collection of All-Stars from one season, various Hall of Famers or players who've accomplished a similar record) the balls don't command much value. Use a baseball encyclopedia to look up rosters from specific years to help determine a baseball's age.

Of course, signed team balls usually should have at least 20 signatures to be valuable. Noted teams, such as the 1969 New York Mets or 1927 Yankees, would be more valued than a ball signed by a last-place team. A baseball missing the autographs of key players from that year's teams (such as Tom Seaver from the 1969 Mets) would be worth less money.

Signed bubble gum cards were discussed in the chapter entitled "What Items Do I Get Signed." In short, signed cards aren't always the best investment vehicle when compared to other autographed memorabilia. Nonetheless, most dealers sell new baseball cards autographed by even the most obscure players at 50 cents each.

Next in line in terms of collectibility and value would be autographed index cards (signed on the unlined side). These cards are bland looking, but are easy to get signed. Collectors have risked no financial loss sending an index card through the mail to a player. For older or deceased players, any signed items might be impossible to obtain. In those cases, "cut" signatures are sought.

These signatures are called "cuts" because they are sometimes trimmed off letters, cancelled checks or envelopes. Many collectors will mat these signatures along with a vintage photograph, creating a nice display item. Paying a high price for a "cut" of a living sports celebrity would be foolish, when other items could be obtained. But a "cut" might provide a classic chance to pick up the autograph of a player who has been dead for years. In 1988, Lelands, a Pennsylvania-based auction house, sold the actual car registration of Lou Gehrig. The document contained a clear signature which read "Henry Louis Gehrig." Considering that he usually signed just "Lou Gehrig," the signature was quite unique.

In recent years, though, collectors have frowned upon "cuts." Instead, they simply collect entire cancelled checks or letters, because these may offer an historical glimpse of the player and provide a comprehensive handwriting sample. A high-ticket collectible would be any handwritten letter from a known star, especially when the content might describe a vital historical event in the player's past.

Try to avoid collecting or purchasing autograph books or yearbooks signed on various pages, unpreserved newspaper clippings, or assorted scraps of paper, because these items won't soar in value. Nor will pencil-signed or other poor-condition autographs be valuable. Personalized signatures lower the resale value of an item but can increase the personal joy a collector finds in the collectible.

Notice that no specific dollar values are given in

this book for any autographs. Why? Because autographs are much more difficult to price than sports cards. Although it's possible to know approximately how many cards of a certain year exist, it's tough to have even a rough guess on how many autographs any given player signed throughout the years. Additionally, regional interest will cause enormous price swings for autographed items. Any New York Yankee, New York Met, New York Giant or Brooklyn Dodger baseball autograph will bring a much higher price in the New York area. Interest in local teams elsewhere would devalue these same signatures in other areas.

For modern era players who are living, always try to obtain the autograph yourself (if possible) to be assured of the signature's authenticity. When it's necessary to purchase an item, try to comparison shop. Scan the advertisements in hobby periodicals. Some dealers will advertise to buy certain signatures at given prices. Thus, if you could buy a signature retail at what other dealers want to pay, you'd be doing well.

Finally, remember that basically no autographs are "one of a kind." Vintage signed materials aren't in great supply, but that's no reason to make a hurried purchase from a dealer asking a skyhigh price. Try to deal with dealers you are familiar with, or ones who have been recommended by other collectors. Again, don't feel the need to collect everything. If a signature is unaffordable for you, it doesn't belong in your collection.

Buying from known dealers who have proven track records can be a help in preventing forged items from appearing in your collection. But more and more forged items appear every day, either from dishonest collectors or from "ghostsigners" who forge autographs for players at the player's request.

Unfortunately, sometimes no person can detect a forgery, not even the autograph signer in question. Hall of Famer Johnny Mize was able to identify a batch of forged autographs using his own name, which had been filtered into the hobby. He admitted that he could not distinguish the masterfully-forged signatures from his own very easily. The only clues Mize used to tell the autographs apart was in the large dot he used in the "i" of his last name. Also, Mize commented that, in player group photos, he would carefully sign his name below the waist on his own image, so he wouldn't clutter the rest of the photo with his signature. The forger would sign Mize's name randomly across the photos.

Autographs obtained by yourself, in person, are guaranteed to be authentic. But in-person autographs may differ greatly from time to time. Try quickly signing your name as many times as possible in one minute. Notice how different the first and last signatures appear. Now imagine how many autographs a sports celebrity might sign for a crowd of fans in just a few minutes. A player's signature might reflect his mood. Former Houston Astros and Toronto Blue Jays catcher Cliff Johnson usually just initialed "C.J." instead of writing his name. Some players may give crisp, detailed signatures when making public appearances, but will only scribble when signing before a big game.

When attending a Wisconsin banquet, I saw two young boys approach an obviously-drunk former Milwaukee Brewers player. This ex-player gleefully tried to sign two autographs, but on each occasion his effort simply turned into a lop-sided scrawl. Still, these were authentic autographs. No collector would ever believe the signatures, though, especially comparing them to the ex-player's normal "sober" signature.

Because some players have nearly-illegible writing all the time, it's wise to keep some sort of identification on the back of the signed item, especially if it's an index card or photograph. Try to include the date when the signature was obtained, too. It's wise to ask these questions of dealers when considering the purchase of an expensive autograph.

Knowing the background of a signed item can help quell doubts about authenticity. It would be strange and suspicious to encounter a dealer from a Midwestern locale like Iowa who would have a baseball signed by Lou Gehrig and Babe Ruth. However, those questions could be answered if the dealer could prove that the ball was obtained while the stars were on a barnstorming tour through the Midwest during the off-season. In the same vein, seeing many Boston Red Sox autographs on the East Coast is likely because more fans there would have asked for autographs from a nearby team. Likewise, it would be reasonable to wonder about a teenager who owned a signed Ruth ball, while a 60-year-old fan might have had more opportunity to obtain this type of item.

Speaking of Ruth, his signature is often forged for two reasons. First, his popular autograph brings a big price, even though he signed often during his career. Secondly, his short name and simple handwriting aren't difficult to copy. A forger might attempt to reproduce Ruth's name on a baseball or photo but may avoid trying to write letters or more complicated tasks. Finding official league balls from this era help prove authenticity because official baseballs weren't available to the public then.

Don't jump to conclusions even if you think you see a dealer at a card show or shop who is selling what appear to be forged autographs. Possibly, the dealer may not have the education to tell real autographs from forgeries. The dealer may have been duped by another dealer. At times, forged items can pass through several channels before being identified. Especially with dated, rarer autographs, authentication is a tricky business.

Always ask about guarantees and return policies when purchasing autographs from unfamiliar dealers. It's fine to ask for photocopies of signatures for sale to help judge authenticity.

The toughest autographs to authenticate today are those of active players obtained by mail. These autographs can be reproduced in three different ways: by rubber-stamp, by autopen, or by using a "ghostsigner."

Rubber-stamped autographs seem to be the most convenient route current players take. Don't think that players always take out their rubber stamps and personally send out bogus replies to hundreds of fans a week. Instead, these non-signing players may never see the mail. A team employee or relative to the player may do the stamping. Rubber stamps are easy to detect. Signatures are often lighter than felt-tip pens. No real indentation is made, and signatures always are compact and rectangular. Rubber stamps will sometimes leave excess dots of ink around the signature area.

One of the worst rubber-stampers in the past was a representative for Milwaukee Brewers first baseman Cecil Cooper. Cooper always declined signing autographs in person at the stadium and would tell fans to write him in the mail instead. When they did, rubber-stamped replies would return. Some would be carelessly stamped on cards so the entire signature did not appear. Who would want a signature which read "Cecil Coo"?

Autopens are tougher to spot. These more-sophisticated devices essentially copy an actual signature of a celebrity. Atlanta Braves star Dale Murphy is one player known to have employed this technique in the past. Again, autopen signatures don't show indentations, and the signature will sometimes show a break or pause between individual letters.

The hardest category to detect is the work of third-party forgers, conveniently termed "ghostsigners" in the hobby. Athletes unable (or unwilling) to answer mail for extended periods of time ask another person to sign autographs in their places. Players tired of constant public attention, players undergoing poor seasons, and those receiving mail at home during the season might turn to forgers. In the case of summer at-home mail, a player's friend or relative may want to reduce the stacks of letters and give fans a prompt reply.

"Ghostsigners" often appear only on a part-time basis. Collectors suspect that some famous athletes may sign some of their mail personally, but pass the rest off to a clubhouse attendant. Players such as Jack Clark, Willie McGee and Vince Coleman have used "ghosts" sporadically in the past. Of course, because both teams and players know that the handling of fan mail is a sensitive public relations issue, all club officials I've ever met insist that players sign all their mail personally. Yet Hall of Famer Mize admits that when he was with the Yankees he saw clubhouse man Pete Sheehy forge autographs for various players.

Networking is one of the best ways to learn about authentic autographs. Try to contact other autograph collectors in person and by mail. Ask about their experiences. Keep good records of your own collecting adventures in person and by mail. Study the forms of authentic signatures. Read autograph articles in hobby publications regularly.

Most of all, don't be afraid to ask other collectors questions. Everyone was a beginning collector once. Almost always, you'll find that knowledgeable collectors will share their wisdom with you.

The Collecting Cavalry: Veteran Hobbyists Come to the Rescue

12

Fans have been collecting sports autographs for decades, long before the coming of Sharpies or ballpoint pens. Incredibly, it took until 1987 for a group of dedicated, veteran hobbyists to come forward and create an organization for sports autograph collectors.

The Universal Autograph Collectors Club is a well-known, long-established organization which has catered primarily to non-sports collectors in many countries. The continued growth of the sports autograph hobby moved Dan Ginsburg, Mark Jordan and Mike Gutierrez to develop a subchapter of the UACC to serve their own collecting needs better. All three men became directors of the UACC subchapter during its founding before officer elections were held.

Gutierrez says that one of the reasons why a subchapter was needed was to protect collectors and dealers alike from forged autographs. The UACC bylaws will provide guidelines so that the authenticity of purchased autographs may be guaranteed for life. "New collectors could do nothing but benefit from membership. In the group, they'd be surrounded by collectors and dealers with good reputations," Gutierrez says. "These club members are people you could get recourse from (if a possibly-forged autograph was sold)."

Currently, U.S. Postal Service laws state that sellers who use the mail must offer a 7-day return privilege if an exchange or refund is desired. However, it could take much longer to determine if an autograph truly is authentic. When collectors like Gutierrez deal in 50- and 60-year-old signatures, authentications can be complex.

That's why the UACC subchapter is developing an authentication committee which can look at questionable signatures. Club members would get these services free initially, then would be charged a small fee for subsequent autograph verifications. The UACC's panel of experts would give combined opinions on autographs. "We'd have more than one opinion to offer," Gutierrez says. "That might stimulate some debate, but debate can be informative."

Why not issue a book to everyone which has authentic reproductions of what Hall of Fame signatures should look like? "We could," Gutierrez says. "We have the combined resources to do a project that big. But we won't. I know of a couple of accomplished forgers out there who'd love to see photocopies to work from. They'd be able to make pencil tracings and forge anyone's autograph."

A photocopy of a signature won't always prove to Gutierrez or club members if an autograph is authentic. "I start from the outside and work in," he says. "I want to see the actual ink of a signature. If it's a Christy Mathewson autograph, I want to see where the ink fades out on the signature. If it's a signed photo, I'll look at the photo first to determine if there's a date or stamp or other clue about the era it came from." Gutierrez says that he's seen forged Babe Ruth autographs penned on illustrations from 1950s era books. Ruth died in 1948.

New collectors would have such hobby knowledge to draw upon regularly. Gutierrez has collected autographs since 1982, and has dealt in autographs on a full-time basis since 1987. He says that he is seeing a rash of forged autographs—of Ruth, Lou Gehrig and anyone who's popular. "Anything can be forged, photos, index cards, whatever," Gutierrez says. "Believe it or not, I've seen two different forged handwritten *letters*, supposedly from Babe Ruth."

The UACC subchapter will do more than help regulate the hobby, Gutierrez says. "We've discussed plans to hold a sports autograph collectors convention. As a part of the UACC, we'd receive some financial support from them." Currently, Gutierrez estimates that only 10 percent of the number of sports memorabilia collectors collect autographs. "If we held a show right now and drew 1,000 people, it would be incredible," he says.

Gutierrez suggests that new collectors away from East and West Coast metropolitan areas could benefit from the communications networks set up with other hobbyists by the subchapter. "In Los Angeles, I met three other collectors immediately when I first started," Gutierrez says. "It isn't so easy to find other collectors when you live in other parts of the country, though." Still in its initial stages, the UACC sports subchapter may be the organization sports autograph collectors have dreamed of for years. Gutierrez says that to be eligible to join the group two other current members must nominate you. Once into the UACC, members will receive the UACC newsletter and a yearly autograph price guide and survey.

To obtain a UACC membership application, contact club treasurer Jeffrey Morey, c/o The Autograph Review, 305 Carlton Road, Syracuse, New York 13207. Be sure to enclose a long, self-addressed, stamped envelope.

Dave Miedema: Portrait of a Star Collector

13

E ver since 1964, at the tender age of five, Dave Miedema has been an autograph collector. A quarter-century and thousands of autographs have passed Miedema since then, but he still fondly remembers his first acquisitions.

"It was just before my sixth birthday," Miedema says. "My dad took me to Wrigley Field. Three Cubs—Leo Burke, Jim Stewart and Dick Ellsworth—signed my scorecard. Ellsworth, who had won 22 games the year before, knew my father, who was a bus driver. Back then, Cubs players could ride the city bus without being hassled."

As a young Chicago resident, Miedema led a charmed life that many autograph collectors would envy. Growing up in the "Windy City," Miedema had access to virtually any National Leaguer at Wrigley Field and any American Leaguer at Comiskey Park, home of the Chicago White Sox. In the late 60s, Miedema used an autograph column in a defunct hobby publication called "Sports Scoop" to obtain home addresses of players. "Jack Smalling had published a smaller address list then," Miedema says. "But it wasn't anything like it is today."

Even back then, Miedema says, some players were using rubber-stamps or ghost-signing tactics to answer fans. "I'd get stamped replies from Hank Aaron, Ernie Banks, Rico Petrocelli and Don Kessinger," he says.

In the early 70s, Miedema discovered the well-guarded secrets of the Chicago hotels which hosted visiting teams. "Media guides were hard to get then," Miedema says. "Instead, I'd call front offices of teams. They wouldn't always give out the information freely, so I might call the Reds and say I was from Ohio and I wanted to stay at the team's hotel when I saw them play in Chicago."

Miedema has stuck with collecting throughout adulthood. He has remained faithful to the hobby even while working as a claims examiner for a federal agency in Chicago. In addition to collecting, Miedema is a part-time sports memorabilia dealer who sells both autographs and game-used equipment. He also writes columns and articles on both subjects for various hobby publications. He says that he receives 75 to 100 hobby-related pieces of mail each week. He offers to answer questions from subscribers of the publications free of charge, a task that is obviously time-consuming.

Shockingly, Miedema has parted with most of the autographs he's received from his younger days. "My collection has sustained semi-frequent purgings," he says with a laugh. "With autograph collecting, I feel that the fun is in the chase." He says that he's condensed his collection at times when "I felt I had everything, or the size of the collection was too immense."

Despite his part-time forays into dealership, Miedema has a sentimental side as well. He says he's most proud of personalized autographs he's received, especially letters from some ex-players. "I'll write to some players and say, 'Sign two of the cards and keep one' as a way of thanking them," he says. "Two men, Dave Melton and Gene Fodge, wrote back and said that no one had ever done that before."

One recent adventure Miedema enjoyed in 1988 was striking up an acquaintance with Oakland A's catcher Terry Steinbach. Miedema wrote about Steinbach in an autograph column for "Sports Collectors Digest" and told how Steinbach was charging for each signature he signed by mail. In turn, all the profits would be used to finance college scholarships. In gratitude, Steinbach sent Miedema an unsolicited signed and personalized 8-by-10 photo. Later, Steinbach had lunch with Miedema when the team played in Chicago.

During his lunch date, Miedema learned again how time changes the signing attitudes of both current and former players. "When I went to lunch," he adds, "I saw Jose Cardenal. He was very nice. When he played for the Cubs and I'd ask for his autograph, he'd just sneer at me."

Miedema has observed lots of other changes in the hobby through the years. "It's getting tougher to get autographs by the team dugout," he says. "In the 1970s, during a mid-week September game at Wrigley, I could get the whole team to sign. In 1988, I went to see the Astros and only got three players." He attributes some of the change to the booming interest in autographs. Hundreds of non-collecting fans suddenly get the urge to meet a player up close, so they use an autograph request as an excuse.

He says that collectors have developed sophisticated tastes over the years. "It used to be that kids

would be thrilled to get anything signed in pencil,"
Miedema says. "Now, the rules are more complex. One
collector wrote to me looking for autographed cards,
only those signed on the front in blue Sharpie. It doesn't
matter how rare the autograph is, or if that player is
dead now."

Another change is in the competition seen at various hotels where players are staying. "Small cities
aren't so rough," Miedema says. "But towns like New
York, Los Angeles and Chicago get competitive."
Miedema says that some collectors trying to get autographs at New York hotels might be harassed by greedy
local collector-dealers.

According to Miedema, he says that out-of-towners
who pay for a room at a visiting team's hotel will fare
best both with local collectors and hotel management.
"Some Chicago hotels play hardball," he says. "I've seen
collectors who disobey hotel rules arrested after
they've been warned." One Chicago hotel forbids collectors from even being on the same city *block* when
trying to get autographs, Miedema says.

During his years as a collector, Miedema has discovered that many players simply dread signing autographs and refuse to do so for any reason. Miedema was
able to get pitcher Mike Marshall's autograph only by
asking a friendly clubhouse attendant to make the request. One star Miedema never got on paper, however,
was the late Yankee catcher Thurman Munson. "I was
never around when he was signing," Miedema says.
"He'd always scream and cuss at people wanting autographs." Miedema says he has found similar attitudes in
second-string players such as Donnie Scott of Texas,
White Sox/Athletics catcher Jim Essian, and Reds/
Royals outfielder Cesar Geronimo.

Miedema points out Charlie Spikes and Jerry Grote as two non-signing players who changed autographing habits later in their careers. "Collectors had a way of getting back at Grote, though," Miedema says. "Sometimes he'd bring his young son with him on road trips. If Grote wouldn't sign, collectors would tease and pick on the boy when they saw him around the hotel."

Unlike many newer collectors, Miedema tries to understand why some players won't sign autographs. "I don't fault the players totally," he says. "Some have the fear of their autographs being resold. Others have more responsibilities, with endorsements and all. And, in the past, players had fewer autograph requests. It's always easier to sign 10 autographs than 100." He feels that a lack of hobby knowledge, not meanness, convinces some players to send back bogus autographs. "I think they don't want the fans to feel ignored," Miedema claims. "They don't try to deceive anyone. They just don't realize that authenticity matters." He says that in the late 70s Joe DiMaggio stopped having his sister, Marie, sign his mail when he learned that collectors objected.

Miedema says that some autograph collectors still have wrong ideas about their hobby. Their first mistake is not including a self-addressed, stamped envelope. Others oversimplify the process of getting autographs. "One reader wrote to me recently and asked me to send back a list of everyone who answers fan mail," Miedema says. "I replied and told him that he was asking too much because hundreds of players will answer by mail." Others can't believe that a player would let someone else sign his mail, Miedema says. "One man wrote and said that he couldn't believe that Dave Winfield won't sign fan mail because he saw him signing at Yankee Stadium. I asked him to send me a photocopy of the Winfield autograph he got by mail. When I sent it back and told him it was a forgery, he was shocked. He said he wanted to stop collecting. I tried to tell him not to take it so hard. Collectors don't realize how many fan letters a star gets each week."

One of Miedema's biggest joys of collecting is sharing the hobby with his wife, Shirley. "Shirley found it intriguing because she had dealt in antiques," he says. "She makes collecting a lot more enjoyable because we can do it together. It's enhanced our marriage."

What keeps Dave Miedema collecting autographs? "The involvement keeps me in," he says. "I enjoy the good friends I've made in the hobby. I'm not a goal-oriented person, because too many goals bring too many disappointments as a collector. I just look forward to how many nice surprises are in store for me."

Hobby Shows Are Heaven for Autograph Collectors

14

T he quickest way autograph collectors can make their collections grow is by attending a sports collector's convention. These affairs vary from day-long informal gatherings in church basements and lodge halls to week-long extravaganzas set in hotel ballrooms or major civic auditoriums.

The process of getting autographs in person from past or present athletic greats who appear at shows was already discussed. The chance to buy other autographs is an overlooked opportunity that can help all sorts of hobbyists, especially those collecting on a budget.

How? Well, time is money. Although a collector might not experience the joy of securing an autograph personally, buying that same signature is a simple, guaranteed way of enlarging a collection. Autograph dealers sometimes approach sports notables and pay them for signing as many as 1,000 autographs in one sitting. Dealers, in turn, acquire huge inventories of autographs and might pass that savings on to collectors who attend hobby shows. Just because a dealer has dozens of autographs of one celebrity, there is no reason to believe that

111

The rules are different at most hobby shows with autograph guests. At an American Legion World Series banquet which featured a signing session, it was possible to take pictures with celebrities. Relief ace Rollie Fingers happily posed for photos with everyone, even me! Ask a show promoter beforehand to see if possibilities like these exist. (Diana Helmer photo)

the dealer forged all of them. Instead, the autographs might be the product of a signing deal.

The most popular autographed product at hobby shows has to be the signed color photograph. Today, it's possible to obtain beautiful autographed photos of hundreds of famous athletes for less than $10 apiece. These photos, many of them vintage poses from early days in a player's career, usually are signed boldly yet legibly in Sharpie marker.

Does this mean that every autographed photo you see at a card show is the result of some athlete who sells his signatures by the truck load? Not really. Sometimes, dealers have gotten the autographs personally, just like any other collector. Often, dealers will receive several free autographs from a show promoter in exchange for renting a table at that show. The dealer may decide to sell these autographs to the public. In other instances, a dealer who lives near a major league team might find an actual team employee willing to help obtain autographs. Therefore, if you meet a dealer from Missouri who specializes in Cardinals and Royals autographs, chances are that the dealer has a local connection with both nearby teams.

The geographical connection is the other likely explanation for how most dealers accumulate hundreds of autographs. If a dealer lives in Seattle, it's possible that lots of fans would want to sell autographs they had gained from the Mariners, the NFL Seahawks and the NBA Supersonics. Due to numerous local public appearances and time spent in one place, it figures that autographs of even the stingiest signers would be plentiful in the cities which host their respective teams.

Geography plays a big part in determining the types of autographs which will be sold at any given hobby show. If a show is held in St. Louis, bet on seeing lots of autographs from St. Louis Cardinals baseball players. This is a mixed blessing for hobbyists searching for Redbird signatures. It's obvious that a wider selection may be found here than at any other shows in the nation. However, an autographed baseball card of someone like Terry Pendleton (which would sell for no more than $1 at other shows) might be priced at $3 or more in St. Louis. Dealers on Pendleton's home turf might inflate their prices due to his local popularity and his success at the time.

Most sports dealers who carry autographs concentrate on signed photos, baseball cards or baseballs. None of these items take up a lot of room at a show. This is crucial for a dealer who is limited to one eight-foot long table. An item like an autographed football or a signed baseball bat would take up lots of room in a dealer's lim-

Hobby shows can provide rare one-on-one meetings between stars and autograph collectors. At a 1988 hobby show in Kansas City, Hall of Famer Lou Brock enjoyed signing and meeting his many fans.
(Diana Helmer photo)

ited display space. Therefore, when dealers do bother with larger items, you can bet that you'll find hefty price tags to boot.

Some dealers realize that an autograph may make a so-so item quite appealing (and worth more money). For instance, dealers who specialize in game-worn team clothing like to sell autographed equipment whenever possible. Having an autograph on a jersey gives the appearance that the item is endorsed as authentic by the player who supposedly once used it. A few sports memorabilia merchants have begun carrying assorted lines of "sports art." An artist will create a portrait of a baseball Hall of Famer or some other sports legend. The portrait will be sold in a limited-edition poster or lithograph form, with each piece signed both by the artist and the featured subject.

Sadly, nearly half the dealers at any given hobby show won't carry any autographs at all. Don't think it's because autographs won't sell well. The real reason is that many dealers don't have any expertise in autographs, and many aren't willing to learn. A few dealers still believe that just because they aren't interested in autographs no one else will be.

On the other hand, uninformed dealers carrying autographs can be just as frustrating to collectors. These hobby hucksters might insist that a team scorecard or yearbook worth no more than $5 should sell at twice that amount if a couple of autographs are found on the cover of the publication. They may try to claim that *all* autographs are rare collectibles. Usually, these fake authorities may not have more than a half-dozen signed items on their tables. A good way to deal with examples of this type of dealer is to ask them if they collect autographs or just sell them. Their greed may reveal itself with a remark such as "I don't sell autographs normally, but I made an exception when I realized how valuable these are."

Before entering any hobby show, it helps to be prepared with a game plan called a "want list." A want list doesn't have to be fancy. It's just a listing which details which particular collectibles you are searching for, be it autographs of only certain players, teams, or certain types of signed collectibles.

Making a want list can help any level of collector in several ways. First of all, it's a good weapon to use when faced with overbearing dealers like the kind discussed above. Your list can detail your goals for the hobby show, along with an estimate of how much you may want to spend on each item. This figure can be arrived at either through your own budget limitations or by the prices you've seen for similar items when advertised in hobby publications.

A little preparation devoted to making a want list can help you enjoy your hobby show visit more fully. Experienced homemakers make a grocery list before they go shopping. Veteran collectors make want lists. Both help avoid impulse buying.

A want list can be a good advertising tool. Try putting your name, address and phone number on the list, then making a few copies of the list before you visit the hobby show. When you go from table to table searching for that one special autograph, offer to leave your want list with the dealer if the dealer thinks he might be able to find that item for you in the future. If a dealer knows that you are a willing and anxious buyer of certain autographs, he'll scout around for your needs at future shows. Then you can complete the transaction by mail. That same dealer might have the autograph you want in his personal inventory but simply neglected to bring it to the show. Dealers have to make lots of tough decisions on what items they'll offer for sale in their limited display spaces at shows.

Communicating your needs to dealers is vital. Take the time to ask each dealer you see at a hobby show if he has autographs for sale. This questioning pays off sometimes when a dealer pulls an extra box out from under his table. Other times dealers who don't have autographs will be kind enough to point you to certain tables that do. Then you're able to save precious shopping time.

Determining the total number of dealers at the show selling autographs is important. This way, there's no need to deal with the first dealer you meet. Granted, you'll find many unique collectibles that may be available only from one source. However, try to find the same item at another dealer's table before making the buy. Compare prices when possible. You'll save in the end.

Now comes the tricky part: making the deal. There are no absolute answers here, for every dealer is a different person with a different business philosophy. The possibility does exist, however, for negotiating a lower price in some instances. Veteran show-goers claim there are two prime occasions to get the best prices from dealers. Sometimes, dealers are more willing to barter during the first hour when a show opens because the dealer wants to clear some early profits before customers spend all their disposable income at other tables. This can work to a collector's advantage, because the selection hasn't been picked over yet.

The other hobby show school of thought maintains that waiting until the *final* hour of a hobby show brings the biggest bargains. Dealers upset with their lack of sales may be willing to cut prices to make some money and to avoid carrying some merchandise back home again. Again, it depends on the individual dealer, his financial success, and his willingness to barter.

In any circumstance, remember that the dealer is very concerned about his image to the buying public. If he agrees to knock $10 off the price of a $50 autographed baseball, it won't be done in front of other customers. Pretty soon, everyone would demand cheaper prices. Because of that dealer fear, it's best to ask for a lower price quietly, at a time when few people might overhear your request.

Furthermore, few dealers will be patient enough to listen to counter-offers if you want to buy less than $10 of merchandise. Basically, show shoppers will find that they get better deals when they buy larger quantities of collectibles from a dealer. With almost any dealer, your initial lower offer will be refused. Veteran dealers will counter with a price approximately halfway between your offer and the original price.

Some hobby newcomers may feel shy about approaching dealers with requests for lower prices. Of course, many offers will be flatly refused. But the effort can be worthwhile if a five-minute conversation can reduce a price by $25. No universal price guide has ever been created for autographs, so few people can truthfully say that they know the real value of any signature.

Breeding loyalty in hobby dealers is a sure way to gain better deals in the future. If you've dealt with a few known dealers who regularly set up tables at a show, they'll try to keep your continued business. Other dealers will learn that you are a serious collector and will try to "lowball" the prices of competitors. So, don't be discouraged if all the dealers you approach insist you pay their full asking prices. The sports memorabilia hobby is growing every day, and every dealer worries about losing customers to competition.

Hobby shows may be great places for buying collectibles, but they aren't so conducive to collector selling. That means that hobby dealers are business people who want to make as much profit as possible when they appear at shows. Although they may sell autographs at certain prices, don't think that they'd buy the same autograph from you at the same price.

Dealers aren't willing to trade in most cases, despite any claims they make. Sure, they say they'll trade with collectors. Their definition of trading means giving the collector no more than 60 percent retail value for the items they wish to trade or sell. Often, you'd have to give a dealer collectibles with an appraised value of $200 to get $100 worth of autographs in return. Before cursing a dealer for this seemingly greedy attitude, remember that this dealer has to invest at least 10 hours a day behind a table, along with expenses for table rental and travel to the show (often from several states away).

The best show alternative for collectors wanting to sell or trade autographs is to participate in show auctions. Some show promoters will plan special auctions in which everyone in the room gets a chance to bid on the available collectibles. The owner, in turn, donates from 10 to 20 percent of the profit as commission to the auction operators.

Sometimes, auctions at hobby shows can provide hidden bargains for collectors. Some show promoters stop show-goers at the door and tell them that, instead of trying to find a single dealer to buy their goods, their items can be put up in an instant auction. This stops certain dealers from trying to monopolize all the walk-in material. However, if most dealers are uninterested in autographs, you might get a lucky bargain.

As I noted in my previous discussions on getting autographs in person, your encounter with the show's celebrity autograph signer may likely be brief. Still, this can be a real highlight of any trip to a weekend hobby show.

Extra research can help uncover other autograph opportunities many collectors might overlook. I'll always remember attending a past hobby show in Des Moines, Iowa. It wasn't the biggest show in the world, nor was the selection the greatest. What I remember most is that, by coincidence, the Indianapolis Indians minor league baseball team was staying there while playing the Iowa Cubs across town. Some members of the team, a AAA affiliate for the Montreal Expos, wandered through the ballroom to check out the event. Some eagle-eyed fans spotted Andres Galarraga (now one of the finest first basemen in the National League). Galarraga was happy to be noticed, and he signed dozens of free autographs. This experience was an instant replay of sorts of the first shows I ever attended in the mid-1970s. These shows, held at the Sheraton Inn in Kansas City, never had a lineup of celebrity guests. Instead, collectors just waited around the hotel lobby. Because the hotel was directly across the street from Royals Stadium, visiting American League teams stayed there. During short weekend stays, I was able to attend a large hobby show and get autographs from the entire roster of the California Angels and Minnesota Twins teams.

Even if it's impossible to stay in the same hotel pro teams do during your hobby show trip, try to tie the journey in with the chance to go see a sporting event. You could still try for some autographs at the stadium. Set your goals high, and be prepared for success. Your next hobby show trip could be the best experience you've ever had collecting sports autographs.

A Talk with Jim Hawkins, Show Promoter

15

Jim Hawkins is one of the most successful promoters of sports collectors conventions known. His shows always provide new opportunities for autograph collectors who want to get in-person signatures either from current Detroit Tigers to stars like Dave Winfield and Ted Williams. As a producer of autograph shows in the Detroit area since 1983, Hawkins has a thorough knowledge of what promoters must do to orchestrate well-run events for collectors and celebrities alike.

An objective attitude towards past and present players might be Hawkins' biggest asset. While some businessmen might feel awkward in the company of an all-star, Hawkins spent 12 years as an unofficial member of the Detroit Tigers. He covered the Tigers throughout the 1970s for the *Detroit Free Press*, traveling with the team from spring training through the World Series.

"During my 12 years with the Tigers, I saw what autograph seekers would subject players to," Hawkins says. "At team hotels on the road, fans would be lurking behind potted palms in the lobby waiting for players to

121

pass by. These collectors would chase them constantly for autographs—in the lobby, the bar when they were trying to relax or the restaurant when they'd be eating." Hawkins says that, as a result, many ballplayers felt that signing any autographs was a nuisance. "Players didn't think of it in terms of resale value then," he adds. "They viewed it more as a personal choice. Back in the early 70s, there was virtually no market for autographs as a commodity."

Hawkins believes that, both then and today, most average players feel flattered to sign autographs. "A lot of players see it as one of their roles," he says. "Fans pay their salaries, so players feel like they need to sign."

After endless hours of hotel lobby sitting with Tigers regulars, and seeing how team stars became reluctant to even venture outside of their rooms, Hawkins gained sympathy for players hounded by the autograph hounds. When he began promoting shows with players as guests in 1983, Hawkins vowed to do things differently.

"I attend to details," he says proudly. "The guys who ran shows in this area before me had total disdain for athletes appearing. Sometimes, they wouldn't even pick them up at the airport, and they had no way of finding the show." Hawkins had fine-tuned his work with players as autograph guests while running "Jim Hawkins' Fan-Attic," a local hobby store. The first guest signer at his store was Tigers manager Sparky Anderson in 1982. "Even though the Tigers were in the midst of a 13-game losing streak, Sparky drew well," Hawkins says. "But when he was done, he refused to take any payment from me. He said he did it as a friend. Jack Morris did the same thing later." Due to the relationships Hawkins had developed as a sports writer, nearly the whole team became his allies as he sought celebrity guests.

Ironically, former Tiger pitcher Denny McLain (who had dumped a bucket of water on Hawkins and another sports writer in a famous lockerroom incident) was the first hobby show guest Hawkins ever signed. The appearance was McLain's first hobby exposure. Now, McLain is a regular on the hobby show circuit.

Hawkins disagrees with the idea that sports notables make hobby show appearances solely for the money. "A lot of today's stars make more than a million dollars a year," he says. "To them, a million isn't a great deal of money. Any offer a show promoter makes them won't be proportionate to what they get paid." Hawkins told how one current player declined his appearance offer recently. "This player, who shall remain nameless, said it wasn't worth his while. The money wasn't a factor. He claimed that he didn't like the attitude of people attending shows, that they demanded friendship after purchasing an autograph ticket. The convenience of the show appearance and the player's current mood usually determine if he'll agree to do the show."

Older players are a different matter when it comes to show appearances, Hawkins says. "Hall of Famers—the older players like Mickey Mantle and Ted Williams—made a pittance compared to what today's players make. These guys want to finally benefit financially from their accomplishments."

Both groups can be troublesome guests if they aren't treated properly, Hawkins says. "Players are accustomed to pampering. It's a fact," he says. "On the road, their itinerary is planned. A team bus is waiting to take them to and from the park, so they don't have to catch taxis. Their luggage is carried for them. They never have to stand in lines." Naturally, they expect show promoters to be just as prepared, Hawkins says. According to Hawkins, "promoters who become fans" fail in this regard. "Some guys putting on shows are on ego trips. They're most concerned with being able to say that they've had dinner with a Hall of Famer."

Few show promoters even turn a profit on autograph ticket sales when a celebrity appears at a show, Hawkins says. "You hope to break even. You're the middle man, the collection agency for the player's fee," he says. Hawkins says that he tries to figure out how many total autographs a guest can sign in the contracted time he appears at a show. Then the total number of autographs is divided into the player's appearance fee to determine the amount Hawkins charges for one autograph.

Hawkins insists that a show containing more than 70 to 80 dealer tables needs a sports personality as an autograph guest to attract both collectors and dealers. "Many dealers base their decisions on which shows to do by the guests appearing at each show," Hawkins says. "Dealers with new material, like 1988 team sets of baseball cards, need a mass audience of hobby novices and kids. Experienced collectors wouldn't be interested." Additionally, Hawkins says that many dealers specializing in older material won't benefit from setting up at an autograph show, because the veteran collectors won't be attracted.

Hawkins says that 99 percent of the collectors who attend his shows to obtain autographs from the guests are happy with his dealings. The few who may complain usually have no understanding of how a hobby show runs.

"Old customers understand, but newcomers may

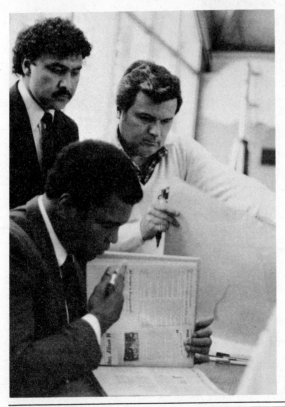

Michigan hobby show promoter Jim Hawkins (center) has attracted some of the top names in sports to his past events. Two notable celebrities who have signed autographs at past Hawkins shows include Kirk Gibson (with beard) and boxing star Muhammad Ali. Always an efficient organizer, Hawkins remains at the side of his guest autograph signer to keep things moving.

not know hobby etiquette," Hawkins says. He says that newcomers may want to pose for pictures with the guests and get personalizations and have brief chats. "I allow those things when there is time," Hawkins adds. "But these people usually want to take time only with superstars like Mantle or Joe DiMaggio. I tell people who complain to me, 'Are you willing to tell the person in the autograph line behind you that they might not get a signature because you want to take extra time?'" Hawkins says that all show guests sign contracts with specific time limitations. Some guests agree to sign only a certain number of autographs, others agree to stay only during a certain time period.

"Collectors have no right to expect anything more than an autograph when they purchase a ticket at a show," Hawkins says. "Guests are there for signing, not smiling, shaking hands and posing for pictures." Hawkins says that fans going to games expect a 100 percent effort from players on the field. Few fans expect good performances to include smiles and waves to the crowd. In the same vein, devoting 100 percent to the signing of autographs may preclude amenities such as shaking hands and posing for photos.

Other problems Hawkins has encountered in the past from fans wanting autographs is the unwillingness of a few to stand in line with everyone else. "Some think they can just walk in and get an autograph immediately," he says. Some people might buy just one ticket then try to get several signatures, which Hawkins describes as "stealing—just like shoplifting off a dealer's table." In cases where a celebrity will only sign a limited number of autographs, the autograph tickets sell out quickly.

Hawkins says that collectors should write or call

promoters beforehand to check on autograph policies. "Ask if advance autograph tickets are available, then buy them if you can," he encourages. "Or, find out what time the day of the show the tickets go on sale, then be there early. Ask if you're limited on the number of autograph tickets you can buy. Look at the show advertisements carefully. Big shows can be overwhelming, so proper preparation is important."

In turn, collectors should expect promoters to make some autograph tickets available during the morning of the show, Hawkins says. Also, promoters should have numbered tickets, which are announced by 50s or 100s. "That way, the line runs well and no one has to stand in line for more than 20 minutes," he adds.

Hawkins won't condemn former players like Joe DiMaggio who rake in thousands of dollars for a mere afternoon of autograph signing. "If DiMaggio signs an official league baseball, valued at $6, it becomes a $50 item once it's autographed," Hawkins says. "These stars read the hobby papers. They know how much their autographs are sold for. Why shouldn't they want a share of the windfall profits?"

The escalating appearance fees do concern Hawkins, though. "We've created sort of a monster with the success of our hobby," he says. "As a player asks for more money for an appearance, the promoter has to raise prices on autograph tickets. I don't know what can be done. Promoters will have to lose money and collectors will have to stop paying high prices for autographs before anything changes. I hope nothing harms the hobby, however."

For more information on the six to eight shows held in the Detroit area each year, send a self-addressed, stamped envelope to Jim Hawkins at 4217 Highland Road, Suite 225, Pontiac, Michigan 48054.

Appendix

For additional information (and to receive current updates on autograph trends) it's best to subscribe to at least one hobby publication. Two general-interest sports collecting publications carry regular features on autographs, while others are devoted solely to autograph collectors.

To learn more about any of these publications, write for current subscription rates and ask how to obtain a sample copy.

SPORTS COLLECTORS DIGEST, 700 E. State Street, Iola, WI 54490. This is a nationally-distributed publication available on many newsstands. This weekly runs a regular column entitled "Up Autograph Alley" by Dave Miedema, along with other occasional articles on autographs. However, baseball cards are the main topics in *SCD*. The publication is valuable for its wealth of advertisements. Buy, sell and trade ads can be a great help to any level of collector. More vintage autographs seem to be sold in *SCD* than anywhere else.

BASEBALL CARD NEWS, 700 E. State Street, Iola, WI 54490. This twice-a-month newspaper carries "Collecting Autographs," a column written by me, Tom Owens. BCN is geared for beginning to intermediate baseball card collectors and contains lots of information on new card sets in each issue. These tips can help autograph hounds come up with new materials to be signed.

SPORTS AUTOGRAPHS, P.O. Box 10190, Marina Del Rey, CA 90295-8864. This newsletter, usually about 12 pages in length, comes out six times a year. The newsletter is a good source for non-baseball mailing addresses. Addresses of other performers, including Olympians, auto racers, golfers and stars from other sports are listed regularly.

JEFF'S BASEBALL NEWSLETTER, Route One, Box 1023, Gerrardstown, WV 25420. This monthly newsletter focuses on collecting Baseball Hall of Fame signatures on Perez-Steele postcards. The newsletter is simply six to eight typewritten sheets, usually with a few pages of photocopied articles. Still, anyone wanting Hall of Fame autographs can glean lots of helpful hints out of each issue. The signing habits of each inductee get close scrutiny each month.

THE AUTOGRAPH COLLECTOR'S MAGAZINE, P.O. Box 55328, Stockton, CA 95205. Also published six times a year, this magazine always features 200 "VIP Addresses." Only a few of the mailing addresses may be of sports stars in each issue. Yet, this magazine tackles offbeat topics ignored by other hobby periodicals. General-interest topics, such as autograph preservation and detection of forgeries, could aid sports autograph hobbyists as well.

THE AUTOGRAPH REVIEW, 305 Carlton Road, Syracuse, NY 13207. This six-times-a-year newsletter is more than a decade old. Each issue is crammed with addresses, most of them sports-related. This newsletter is a true forum for collectors. Editor Jeff Morey publishes all reader feedback, and the sharing of collecting information creates a helpful, entertaining publication.

Any or all of these publications can be excellent resources for collectors. Don't stop with a subscription to one of these. Correspond with other hobbyists. Run periodic advertisements to buy, sell or trade with others. Share the news of your collecting setbacks and triumphs. Your active participation will make our hobby even more fun and satisfying.